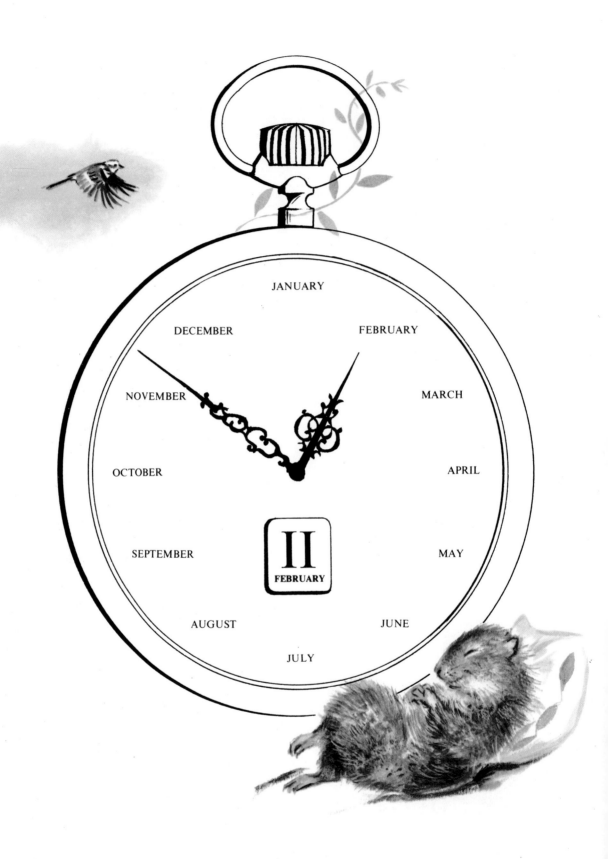

ANIMALS
Around the Year

By Marcelle Verité

Translated by Melville M. F. Wallace

Illustrated by Romain Simon

GOLDEN PRESS · NEW YORK

Western Publishing Company, Inc.

Racine, Wisconsin

Foreword

This beautiful book from France explores how animals live naturally throughout the year. Some of the animals will be familiar to you, and can be seen from your own window or in your own park or garden. Others will be strange: some are wild, and found only in the forests or mountains of Europe.

But each of them—from the tiny ladybird beetle to the great horned owl—is fascinating. And each plays its role in maintaining the balance of nature.

If man does not intervene, this balance is not upset. If, for instance, the mouse population swells for one reason or another, the tawny owls will lay more eggs and soon, because there are more birds of prey, the number of rodents will diminish. If, on the other hand, the food on which the mice live is in short supply and their numbers drop, there will be a corresponding drop in the number of owls living in the neighborhood.

As you read this fascinating treasury of animal facts and lore, you will be learning about the habits and habitats of many different animals at different seasons of the year. You will learn how the birds celebrate the coming of spring, watch them take their summer baths and follow them during the wintertime as they hungrily search for food. And if some snowy day you notice scarlet berries on a barren branch, you'll remember that these plants need the birds to spread and fertilize their seeds.

As you read, you will notice that animals are subject to strong drives. The first is, of course, the need to eat, and this frequently makes them leave their homes and travel from one part of a country or continent to another.

Another strong drive is the urge to reproduce, and it is this that motivates many animals, fish, and birds to travel hundreds and even thousands of miles so they may nest where they themselves were born.

Many animals spend all their lives moving about, and many others build homes that last a long time.

But you will see that most animals, whether or not they build homes, usually live within certain boundaries—an area that they consider theirs. This area may be very small (for instance, the distance a sea bird can strike with its beak while sitting on its nest) or it may be very large (a bear's domain may cover many miles). But while each family has its own territory, and will defend it against others of the same species, they are perfectly willing to share it with other kinds of animals.

As month follows month in this book, you will learn a great deal about all of these animals. Yet they will still keep much of their mystery, for it takes a great deal of curiosity and hours of patient watching to uncover their secrets.

The lives of animals are always exciting and frequently dangerous. The stories we tell of them here are but stories, of course, but they reflect knowledge it has taken years of observation to record. But remember, the book of nature is never closed—it will be up to you to write its next pages.

Contents

WINTER

Blackbird

Thrush

Nuthatch

JANUARY

New Year Mistletoe

As the winter garden sleeps peacefully under its blanket of snow, a raucous cry suddenly pierces the silence and dark, flapping wings fly down from the ivy-covered wall. It is a blackbird come to breakfast on the small dark clusters of berries.

But another bird has beaten it there: a hungry thrush pecks at the berries, wings fluttering as the slim stalks bend under its weight.

Wary of the contest, the thrush soon beats a retreat to its usual haunts—the old apple trees in the orchard. The mistletoe plants that grow on the branches there serve as its private larder. Greedily pecking at the white, translucent berries, the bird unknowingly carries one to a nearby branch; later, it will sprout there. Like the jays who bury acorns and beechnuts for their winter food supply, thrushes also help distribute seeds.

Suddenly the whole garden comes to life. Whistling as it works, a small blue-gray nuthatch scurries up a tree trunk, exploring every nook and cranny with its long curved beak for the juicy insects hidden here and there.

Hare and bird tracks in the snow

Now it is the green woodpecker's turn. Flying off to his favorite tree, he sends out a warning shriek that echoes like a bugle blast throughout. Then to work: toc-toc-toc; he picks away at a hollow trunk in search of insect delicacies.

A small warbler, feathers ruffled to keep out the cold, hops about in underbrush where the snow could not penetrate.

Nobody heeds the arrival of a slim, furry creature who daintily lifts its feet and arches its back as if to avoid soiling its pretty fur. Is it a cat, with its pointed ears and pink muzzle, just back from a hunting expedition in the still sleeping forest? No, it's a marten—an elegant fellow with dark boots, a smooth chestnut coat and a long tufted tail. His shining eyes see and remember everything that goes on in the half light.

Perhaps he is looking for a squirrel's nest, for he is a flesh-eater. Many a time he's tracked down these acrobats of the treetops who make their win-

Green woodpecker   Robin

ter nests in the forked trunks of old trees. Or he may breakfast on juicy berries, for he enjoys fruit, too. But the important thing right now is to leave no tracks in the snow that could be followed by men.

Here, some crows have passed by, and a hare has left the print of his long paws, five toes in front and only four behind. And these star shaped marks are the signs of sparrows, robins, tits, wrens and buntings. But even before the pale sun rises over the horizon, the marten will turn his light little steps toward the old oak tree where he makes his home. There, in his favorite snug quarters, he will sleep the day through rolled up into a ball, his sharp nose buried in his magnificent fur coat, dreaming, perhaps, of feasts to come.

Stalking daintily through the snow, the beady-eyed marten sees everything and forgets nothing.

A mound of dirt on the snow marks the entrance to the mole's home.

The Mole in the Garden

A thin blanket of snow covers the meadow. But look! There in the midst of this vast, white expanse a little molehill has appeared overnight.

Don't moles sleep during the winter? They would hardly deny the fact, but here is the evidence—they have been at work. Of course, it is very unlikely that in winter you will ever actually see a mole. And even in mid-August, when water becomes scarce, you're lucky if you can spot them rushing from their hideaways to a nearby stream or pond. (After all, eating three times a day—or even more often—can give you quite a thirst!)

But it is only January now, and the appearance of a molehill on the meadow means that Mr. Mole has been busy. What a strange creature he is—round as a sausage with a blunt pink nose, tiny black eyes no bigger than poppy seeds and as awkward as he is quick. He spends vitually all his life underground, incessantly pushing ahead with his nose and digging endless burrows with his huge, powerful forepaws, each of which is equipped with ten strong claws. Moles eat whatever they come across, but prefer insects. Like hedgehogs (and shrews), they belong to the insectivore family, and with 44 dagger-sharp teeth are admirably equipped to pierce insects' armor and slice them up (rather than grind them down). As each mole eats the equivalent of its own weight every day, idleness would not only be a sin, but a matter of life and death as well. In fact, it is said that moles die if they have to fast for twelve

Mole cricket

Cross section of a mole's nest

hours. In any case, with such appetites, they must be ever on the lookout for food. In the process, they can dig almost 50 feet of tunnels per hour, a figure which gives some idea of the strength of their powerful claws. And they tunnel even faster in springtime when they are looking for mates.

Moles are essentially unsociable, living alone and resenting all intruders. However, mother moles take good care of the tiny, blind and hairless offspring that are born in the depths of their underground nesting chambers. Generally hidden under walls or a tangle of roots, these hideaways always have an escape hatch and connect with surrounding tunnels.

Moles are cautious, and have few if any friends. Even the largest grass snake hesitates to slither inside a mole's tunnel, and wily martens show the same prudence.

Of course, molehills are a nuisance, particularly to the gardener, but we must remember that in all their tunneling activities, moles do far more good than bad: they aerate the soil much deeper than any earthworm, and in their passage they destroy not only healthy roots, but also insect eggs, cocoons and larvae, as well as caterpillars and worms. Moles have such an enormous appetite for earthworms that there are never enough to satisfy them, however fast they multiply.

Although moles don't seem to like the white worms which gobble up lettuce and strawberry plants, they do get rid of another root cutter: the mole cricket. The mole cricket is a serious insect pest in parts of Europe.

Thanks to moles, flowers bloom more profusely in the spring.

A mole can tunnel almost 50 feet in an hour.

JANUARY

The Alpine Raven

Across the Alpine valleys a harsh, piercing cry rings out in the frozen dawn: "Koaarp!"

The great Alpine raven seems to rise with the sun, casting his great shadow over the landscape just as the sun gilds the snow-capped peaks with its rosy mantle.

How black the huge bird looks against the blue of the winter sky! Not until the sun's rays touch his enormous wings (spanning 1½ yards) do we notice the iridescent glints of blue, vermillion, purple and green in his plumage.

Suddenly he dives vertically into the valley, rises again, then loops and spins to limber up a bit. After all, twenty years of living is a long time, even to a great raven.

If he could only speak, what stories he could tell of his life in the mountains! How many marmots, hare, birds and wild, goatlike chamois and ibex has he seen pass by below! And heaven only knows how many lambs, how many weak or ailing animals he has torn asunder with his sharp beak. Scavenger of the slopes and steep ravines, he eats just about everything—fish, weasels, rabbits, eggs and even fruit. And sometimes, in the spring, just to sample the season, he will even nibble on a few new shoots of grass.

With such a rich and varied diet, remarkable eyesight and the dutiful wife who each year, in mid-March, sits over the next raven generation in their forest nest above a flowing stream, is it any wonder that he feels so well in his ripe old age?

Here he comes now, slowly flapping his wings, his enormous beak splitting the heavens with an awful noise. At last he lands behind the closed and shuttered bar on the top of a cable car for skiers. Then, after making sure that he is alone, he strides majestically to—the garbage cans! A sinister black shape darkens the sun, casting a cross-shaped shadow on the snow below. It is Mrs. Raven coming to join her husband for lunch.

She turns her head right and left as if checking the possibility of live game, but there's no sign of a tit's flashing wings. Even the eagle will probably not come too close, for he, like other birds of prey, prefers to avoid the noisy ravens.

Do ravens have no enemies, then? None to worry about—except perhaps the fearless great horned owl, and he only sets out on his downy wings at nightfall when the ravens have gone home to roost.

Mr. and Mrs. Raven lunch amply and well on garbage. Now that skiers have invaded these slopes, there is always a ready meal available.

In the tall pines, goldcrests eke out their living as they watch the winged giants soaring overhead, unaware that they are cousins, members of the large passerine family. After all, it would take two hundred of them to match the weight of just one of the great ravens.

Ravens feasting

"Koaarp, koaarp!" Again the raven's hoarse, wild cry floats out over the mountains. As the first car on the cable starts its ascent, Mr. and Mrs. Raven scan the horizon for a south-facing rocky crag where they can roost comfortably while they watch the skiers on the snowy slopes.

Perched on a towering rock, the Alpine raven warms himself in the sun and surveys his domain. Soon he will lunch on whatever the skiers have left behind.

To Sleep Is to Dine

In mid-January the garden seems deserted, and twice as lonely as the nearby forest itself. Yet here and there tiny hearts beat steadily in the furry breasts of many sleeping creatures.

The squirrel, for instance, slumbers cozily in his little hut. He built it himself in an old magpie nest and improved it with bits of moss and twigs carefully combed into place by his fine-clawed paws. He is happy there, his head neatly tucked under his bushy red tail, sleeping the winter away. It could be said, of course, that "to sleep is to dine," but when the weather warms up a bit, the squirrel will wake up and check his larder. He will look for the tender mushrooms he hid under the moss last fall, or the tasty hazelnuts stored between cracks in the bark of his tree, or perhaps the chestnuts whose spines stung

This little red squirrel is using an abandoned magpie's nest for his winter home.

Edible dormouse

Garden dormouse

his paws when he gathered them. Will he remember where they all are?

In a nearby walnut tree, the little edible dormouse rests all curled up in a leafy, moss-filled nest, his tiny paws clutched into fists. Though not so fluffy as a squirrel's, his tufted tail is still long enough to wrap around and warm his little pointed nose. This fruit-loving rodent won't wake up for many a day. He'll sleep on like a groundhog. And so will his two smaller cousins, the garden dormouse (who also nests in walnut trees) and the graceful, tiny common dormouse.

By nature nocturnal, these mouselike little fellows are rarely seen even in good weather, but the havoc they wreak in orchards is all too visible; they have the nasty habit of starting to eat fruit without ever quite finishing the job. As they are very timid and cautious, much of their lives remains a mystery. Nevertheless, owls and nightprowlers (such as the lean, long-bodied weasels and winter-starved mar-

tens) will undoubtedly turn up a few here and there.

Lurking in his lair is still another enemy, but this is not the season for him to attack. The cold-blooded viper hates sunshine, but winter's cold merely makes him drowsy. Now he slumbers on in his cool lair, and when he finally wakes he won't have far to go in order to find a satisfactory meal of slugs and worms.

Still another drowsy reptile snoozes peacefully in the chinks between two stones under the ivy-covered, crumbling wall. Even in January, an unexpected burst of sunshine may lure the gray lizard out for a few minutes' warmth (though he will rush right back and not show his nose again for many a day).

Today, however, the cruel wind blows in gusts, shaking tree limbs in the overgrown garden where all these tiny creatures peacefully sleep, awaiting the finer weather to come.

Viper

Gray lizard

Tawny owl

Eagle owl

Vole

Field mouse

An Evening in January

Ruffling his feathers on this frigid, dreary January night, the eagle owl seems twice his normal size as he preens his feathers one by one. This nocturnal bird of prey has dark feathers mixed with russet on his back, fine white down on his breast, and tufts, or "horns," on his head that hide his invisible, sharp-tuned ears.

These ear-tufts are worn by almost all the great owls, although smaller species such as screech or barn owls are without such decoration.

Throughout the day, the eagle owl had been sitting quite motionless on a limb, his eyes half shut. Yet despite his sleepy appearance, he was wide awake; he was merely shielding his eyes against the daylight's glare. Like all birds of prey, his eyes are fitted with a protective membrane.

Hare

And now that night has fallen, he is still on the lookout for a weasel or a vole. In fact, having fasted for three days, he wouldn't scorn the tiniest field mouse, but, unluckily for him, they and the dormice are deep in their lairs, the rabbits in their burrows and the hares well hidden (and always alert).

Suddenly the sound of sharp claws can be heard grating against the frozen ground, and the eagle owl snaps wide his flaming orange eyes.

That furtive shape sneaking under the lowermost branches is his sworn enemy, the fox. And the fox's lady is nearby, too, sniffing beneath a pine.

The forest holds its breath, for these two—the bird of prey and the fox—are bound to fight. Their rivalry is all the more deadly as game is so rare at this time of year.

Spreading his wings over his head, back arched and feathers ruffled, the bird of prey swoops furiously to the attack.

With his very life threatened, the fox holds his ground, yellow eyes defying the onrushing orange crescents, his fangs bared against the descending beak and cruel, curved claws.

This time the battle ends almost as soon as it began—in a draw.

A few wisps of downy feathers and a few red hairs drift in the air, then float gently to the ground.

Back arched, wings spread overhead and eyes flaming, the eagle owl dives down on his mortal enemy, the fox.

That is all. Furtively, the adversaries slink away in opposite directions to resume their nighttime hunting.

"Whoo-whoo, whoo." From time to time the eagle owl calls out across the forest, and from the depths of a ravine his mate replies with softer cries—strange sounds ringing out across the frozen silence.

Downy wings slide noiselessly between the poplars, and a crow, foolish enough to show himself before the great birds of prey, is snatched up and devoured without a sound. So much for dinner!

On this frosty night the twigs twinkle as if they were stars and the forest slowly goes back to sleep. Still, in the darkness, the hare remains hidden, listening to the hostile silence, fearful of leaving his lair before dawn lest he be betrayed by his shadow in the moonlight. Yet if he can only manage to survive until spring, he will once again while away the sunny afternoons under the forest's green canopy.

Then, beneath the nest where the owl has brought up her young, the remains of rodents, reptiles and vermin will show that the birds of prey are indeed friends of man and have done us many a favor.

21

The Birth of a Baby Lamb

The mother sheep had spent the summer in the Alpine meadows under a canopy of stars and a shepherd's watchful eyes. The few lambs who had been born there in the mountains before the shepherd decided that it was time for the flock to come down made the trip in baskets hung on both sides of a sure-footed ass.

Up north it was still bleak wintertime, but here on the plains of Crau, a lowland area of southeastern France swept by warm winds from the Mediterranean, the sun shone and the almond trees would soon be in blossom. Nibbling at the sparse grass growing between the pebbles, the ewes browsed along. (Only rarely does the flock spend a whole day inside the shelter of their tile-roofed fold, though they return to the pens nightly.)

Now, at lambing time, the shepherds hardly have time for sleep. Every night sweet little lambs with soft pink hooves are born to give pleasure to their mothers.

Within the dark sheepfold the warm and delicious aroma of milk and fleece fills the half-light.

In the evenings, snowflakes dance across the plains and the air becomes icy and crisp. On such a night, one ewe gave birth to a son, a superb little lamb with lacy ears, his soft coat all tightly-curled ivory.

Holding the newborn in his arms, the shepherd gazed at him proudly. To think that even at this age he already had tiny horns! At this rate, he'd grow to be a rugged beast with formidable horns, curled like snail shells; perhaps he'd even become the leader of the flock.

Now, however, he was only a tiny white bundle with dark, plaintive eyes.

As if he were speaking to the shepherd, the newborn let a pitiful bleat escape his velvet lips. His mother replied tenderly, and somewhat anxiously, so the shepherd set her offspring back down on the ground. The lamb could barely stand on his wobbly legs, but lifting his head he quickly found his mother's warm milk and began to nurse.

Outside, frost covered the plain. An icy wind bent the cypress trees and whistled through the roof tiles, yet mother and son were cozily warm within and undisturbed by the storm raging outside.

Certainly it was no time for little lambs to venture out of doors; they would have to wait for better weather before going forth to nibble the tender grass, and even then, never leave the fold before the sun had dried the dew.

Then, about May or June, when the heat becomes stifling and the grass thin and tough, it will be time for the flock to quit the valley once again for the lush pastures of the Lower Alps. As usual, they would follow those narrow paths up the crests that had been cut out by countless generations of sheep before them. Sure-footed and safe from marauding wolves, they would make their way to the heights. (Contrary to popular belief, eagles do not swoop down to carry off little lambs.)

But spring has not yet come, and there is plenty of time for the little ram's horns to grow. Now he sleeps softly beside his mother.

After a summer on the high pastures, the sheep return to the warm fold for winter; here fleecy white lambs are born.

Tawny owl

From a nearby wood, her husband's sudden soft hooting startles thrushes and blackbirds, but Mrs. Owl merely turns her heard 180 degrees in response to the call. And turn her head she must, for her eyes always point straight ahead. Five seconds of silence, and then again the soft "hou-hou-hou" rings out.

This time of cold and snow and frosty air is the tawny owl's mating season, and both are thinking of their downy nest in a hollow tree.

But it is dinner time . . . .

From the threshold of the barn, the farmer's cat hesitates before gingerly stepping out into the snow to greet the owl with a plaintive meow. They have little in common, these two, except perhaps that in

FEBRUARY

The Barn Owl

How does the tawny owl know when dormice are hidden beneath the haystack?

All birds are sharp-eyed, and the goshawk can spot prey on the ground from a height of 700 feet. Yet the tawny owl, whose black agate eyes cover most of its face, has no need to soar to such an altitude or even cruise over the fields to know instinctively where dormice are hiding. Having lived in the same old ivy-hung apple tree for so many years, the tawny owl has learned a great deal about the ways of beasts and birds.

And in the rugged month of February, when snow covers the ground and the little rodents stay at home, she keeps a watchful eye on the haystack, her private larder. Motionless but alert on her limb she watches and waits.

he dark their eyes reflect every ray of light, though their vision is not so extraordinary as is commonly supposed.

Yet these twilight hunters respect one another, knowing they hunt the same game—fledglings, rodents and even baby rabbits.

Mrs. Owl ruffles her feathers until she looks exactly like a ball of fluff sitting on two legs, and her beak retreats into the feathered mass. She makes no reply to her husband's call, which by now has developed a plaintive note. After all, he would rejoin her on their bough within the hour. The cat looks up inquiringly, as if to ask: "What are you waiting for?" But the bird has decided to act, and swift as a bullet dives down onto the haystack. There is a moment's flurry, a few small, strident cries, and then she reemerges with a little mouse hanging from her talons.

"Hou–hou–hou. . . ."

She's found her evening meal.

Yes, the haystack has lost one of its inhabitants. But for each one lost, ten more will appear. There is no point in scolding the farmer's friend; she deserves praise instead.

The cat watches the downy-winged bird return to her bough, then wends her way back to the barn as evening falls.

Making slow patterns in the winter sky, the tawny owl keeps an eye open for furtive voles.

FEBRUARY

The Great Stag

With measured step a tall and elegant beast makes stately progress along the forest path between the beeches. The great stag is leaving his lair among the thickets. He is hungry, and snowflakes dot his gray-brown winter coat that is interspersed with white down. Frost has formed a little beard beneath his black muzzle, and his long-lashed eyes turn in the direction of his mate, who leads the herd. Across the ferns she looks back, knowing the ways of her forest knight. She'll only see him again in the fall when his blood burns with fever, or perhaps during some desperate time when hunger overrules all.

She knows that he will be leaving them toward the end of the month, that alone and apart he will lose the antlers nobly crowning his brow, and that he will only reappear again when the leaves start to fall and his hoarse voice thunders out at night across the glades.

The young does shiver, lifting their heads uneasily as they chew the crisp, frozen ivy leaves. They have exhausted the resources of the deep forest and must now make do with whatever is left: the tender bark of oak and chestnut and the bitter twigs of bushes.

Coming to a decision, the old doe sets off, her muzzle set against the wind. The rest of the herd follow Indian file, last of all the old stag with head held high. The cracking of twigs under their dainty hooves echoes across the frozen ground.

Elusive as smoke they trot through the scrub and the patches of heather, their sleek coats glistening and their warm breath rising like steam from their flaring nostrils.

They will not waste their strength in aimless wandering, for the old doe remembers a sheltered spot where a stream flows silently beneath a thin film of ice; last summer they feasted there on crisp watercress.

Under the spreading oak trees which just now are losing their last leaves, the wild boar (a kind of wild pig) have cut deep grooves in their frantic search for a downy field mouse's nest or a few acorns. And here and there is an outcrop of white lichen like those that the reindeer of Lapland feed on in the wintertime.

Stages in the growth of a stag's horns

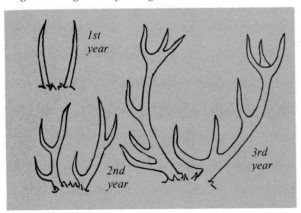

1st year

2nd year

3rd year

Pawing the ground, the stag can uproot a few weeds here, a tuft of dried grass there, and then he must be content with more bark. Sometimes, he stands erect and motionless, sniffing the air and glancing at the old doe who is also momentarily on the alert. Then they both resume their browsing, for all is quiet.

When the long winter night falls over the barren oak trees, it is time to return to their lair. Perhaps tomorrow the leader of the herd will leave them. The days are getting longer, but only a little thrush, calling sadly from a woodpile, is aware of this. Snowflakes once again swirl in the darkness, white shadows melting into the frozen landscape.

27

FEBRUARY

The Bee

In each beehive there are three kinds of bees: a queen bee (who lays eggs), drones (one of whom will mate with the queen), and workers. In a hive of 10,000 bees, there are at least 9,500 workers. And now, at the first sign of sunshine, it is these bees who take to the air in search of flowers.

But can you guess what kind of flower dares show itself this early in the year?

There are the buds of the willow and hazelnut tree, tiny daisies and other early flowers like the lesser celandine, or pilewort, which spreads out yellow satinlike petals.

In the hive, the queen bee begins to lay her next brood. The larvae need honey, fresh pollen and plenty of water to melt the honey which has been crystalized by the cold. This mixture makes their favorite porridge.

Bees are perfectly willing to make long flights just to gather up a few drops of dew; but at this time of year, there isn't any dew! Fortunately, the owner of the hive knows his business and has provided a bag of crystallized sugar moistened with water.

The bees come and go, bringing their harvest of pollen in little "baskets" in their hind legs. Returning from their last trip, however, the bees find the hive in a hubbub.

For the past few days, a green woodpecker has come regularly to test the strength of their wooden house. Toc-toc and tap-tap, he has finally succeeded in drilling a little hole and has rudely helped himself to honey, bees, eggs . . . and even wax!

It's just lucky that the field mouse is still sleeping and so hasn't taken advantage of the hole to further diminish the bees' supplies. When he finally awakes in the spring, there is a good chance that the bees now so busy will be dead.

Though the queen bee's life may last from three to five years, the worker bee's life is short. Sometimes it lives less than two months. But how industrious it can be in that brief time!

As a young worker, it tidies up the cells in the comb, distributes pollen and nectar within the hive, builds new rows of cells, and stores provisions brought in by older workers. It also stands guard, checking each visitor's identity with its long antennae and ruthlessly driving off intruders. (Sometimes, if a little mouse cannot be forced out, he is unceremoniously coated with wax!)

After two or three weeks at such chores, our worker bee will spend the remainder of its brief life gathering pollen and nectar for the hive.

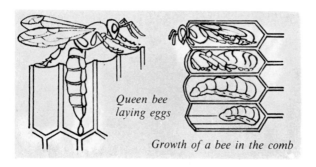

Queen bee laying eggs

Growth of a bee in the comb

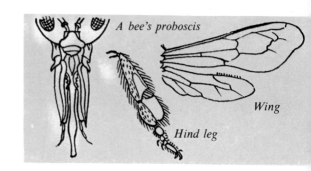

A bee's proboscis

Wing

Hind leg

The queen bee is constantly fed by her subjects; her only job is to lay as many eggs as possible.

Sometimes a worker may appear to be pointlessly hopping about at the entrance to the hive, but actually, by sounds and gestures, the bee is telling its co-workers where the pollen-bearing flowers are (the bee's odor seems to transmit a message too).

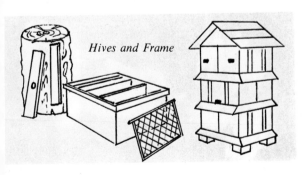

Hives and Frame

Now, however, our bee has but a few days left to live. Soon we will no longer see it buzzing back from the orchard covered with red or white pollen, nor returning from the fields bearing the fine black dust from poppy stamens. When the smell of apple blossoms fills the air, other bees will have taken up its tasks.

Thousands upon thousands of flowers must be visited to produce just a couple of pounds of honey, and the hive will hum with activity until the last autumn aster falls. Then it will remain dormant throughout the winter.

But let us thank the bee for its good work, not only for the delicious honey it provides but because, in seeking it, the bee carries pollen from one flower to another and thus fertilizes our orchards.

29

However gloomy things may seem, the seasons are changing and spring is just around the corner. Though sometimes their nests are still covered with snow when the stork returns, how welcoming they must seem from a distance. Up close they're nothing more than a disorganized jumble of sticks, with here and there a few feathers, bits of grass, old rags

FEBRUARY

The Storks Return

Returning storks are a sure sign of spring. Once last year's nest has been rearranged, the stork couple remains inseparable throughout the season.

Tender young leaves are still hiding within their tough-shelled buds when the storks fly overhead. Every year, toward the end of February, European newspapers carry stories about the storks' return from their winter sojurn in Africa, but just as a single swallow doesn't make a summer, so the storks are unable to bring the African sunshine with them. Their presence up north doesn't mean that summer will come early any more than their departure in mid-August indicated that the coming winter would be cold. Like all migrating birds, they obey immutable laws which send them northward to their birthplace where they themselves will nest, and then southward toward those sun-drenched lands where they can comfortably avoid the bad weather.

Mr. Stork usually precedes his wife by several days, and the sight overhead of his shining wings, tapered body and straight neck (unlike the S-curved neck of flying herons) brings joy to every heart.

or paper. No matter! The nests will soon be repaired, and then defended against those lazy birds who would rather appropriate them than build their own. Battles can occur—and when they do, beaks flash and feathers fly!

Finally, Mr. Stork can settle in. Perched high up on a steeple (he likes to look out over the countryside), standing on his skinny, bright red legs and pointing his vermillion beak toward a sky dotted with downy clouds, he awaits his lady love.

And here come the female storks, flying in a great circle. One will separate and glide slowly down as the others continue their journey. Mr. Stork greets his mate's arrival at their nest with many bows and clackings of his huge beak, and the fact that he cannot utter a chirp doesn't mean that he cannot be polite. Whenever either stork comes back to the nest he is always greeted with ceremonial bows and noisy clacking. (Though storks love each other tenderly and behave with unfailing courtesy to one another, their devotion does not mean they will remain united for life, but only for one season.) After the first shining white egg is laid, Mrs. Stork will remain in the nest until three or four more appear. Mr. Stork, too, will take his turn at keeping them warm, and later he'll act as an umbrella to shield the fledglings. The babies' first meals will be a stew of june bugs and other insects, and later they'll be brought tiny mice and frogs—which will gradually increase in size as their own size increases. And soon enough they'll be gobbling up the still-quivering snakes that their fond parents bring.

At the tender age of three weeks, little storks start flapping their wings, and only ten days later, encouraged by their parents' incessant example, they too launch themselves into the air. Then, after a mere two weeks, they will leave the nest forever.

MARCH

The Pike's Picnic

Birds have left the sunny shores of Africa and returned to northern climes; the weather is improving.

But other new arrivals are more to the liking of the pike, a large carnivorous fish commonly found in European rivers. In long files, tiny eels, or elvers, are making their way up the Loire River in central France. But are these barely visible creatures weighing only one-thousandth of a pound really eels? Indeed they are, and they've come a long way already, for they have spent up to three years swimming here from their birthplace in the Sargasso Sea, thousands of miles away in the middle of the Atlantic Ocean.

The pike, who had passed the winter dozing on the bottom of the river, thrills at the sight of them. He knows that elvers only swim at night and that by day they remain hidden in the sand. This gives him the chance to gobble them up by the thousand—a third of his own weight every day, in fact—and then digest them at leisure under some half-sunken bough. When he was young, he was called "the knife-handle, "the whistle," or "the dagger," and even today, at the ripe age of fifteen, he has kept his slim figure, and the shovel-like snout which hides rows of steel-sharp teeth. Soon the elvers will be gone, and then the pike will use his speed and fighting trim to catch other game, above all his favorite, the gudgeon, a small freshwater fish.

As he does much of his hunting by stalking his victim, and as he can remain motionless in one spot for hours, he succeeds in catching a wide variety of prey. With eyes well on top of his head, he can see what is going on even while lying on the river bottom. All he needs is one glimpse, and then off he swims like a living torpedo. He will eat almost anything that swims: his own young, the frogs near the banks and whatever the spring waters bring downstream—larvae, insects, half-drowned mice or rats. When the ducks have their fledglings, he rises stealthily to the surface to grab the little ones.

The pike is a pirate, that much is obvious, but in killing off everything within his reach, he also does away with weaklings and the diseased, and thus prevents epidemics.

People usually fish for pike in the summertime when pike enjoy warming themselves under the

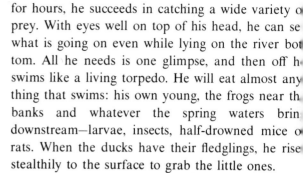

Eel

Pike

nlight in still ponds. But getting a pike to shore is
o easy matter! Fishermen will tell you how often
ike have snapped their lines as if they were
reads. After all, fifteen years is a long time in
hich to learn tricks.

Fishermen also claim that pike do not feed every
ay, or even at the same time of day, but that,
ddly enough, all of the pike in a certain stretch of
ver will "bite" together at roughly the same time.

When a pike gets hooked, he doesn't give up
ithout a serious fight. But the pirate is a catch
orth having, who often enough concludes his exis-
nce on some gourmet's table. But by then, of
ourse, other "knife-handles," "whistles" and "dag-
rs" will have taken his place in the still waters of
e Loire.

MARCH

The Field Mouse and the Bumblebee

A field mouse who had passed the winter in the stable now sat on the edge of the Thoroughbred's stall. Vigorously rubbing his nose and smoothing down his long whiskers, he decided it was time to go back to the fields.

Like other members of his vast family, he had spent the winter comfortably indoors in barns and attics, living off others' provisions but never touching a single one of the poisoned pellets put out for him by the farmers. The only thing he had had to worry about during the winter was roaming cats.

Having feasted on the chickens' stores of golden corn and the horses' oats, he felt very fit, and his sleek coat and well-rounded form testified to his good health. Like any other rodent, his main problem was to find a way to wear down his teeth, for they grew all the time. So, each time he ploughed through some new path to suit his purposes, he gnawed away constantly at whatever wood was handy.

Content though he'd been here, this mouse knew spring was coming, and so he set out toward the fields. Sticking close to the hedges under which nettles sprouted, he made his way through tufts of wild flowers.

In a leaf-filled ditch along the way, he encountered a hedgehog on the prowl for slugs and worms. Quick as a wink he slipped out of sight.

Barely had he regained his breath when he charged into the path of a viper that was unwinding its coils in the sun at just the spot where he wanted to slip under the fence into the meadow.

As luck would have it, however, this problem was lved by a hunting scops owl who found the uirming snake far more tempting than the ouse's dun-colored coat. Frightened almost to ath, the mouse ran under a piece of bark. When raised his trembling head, he saw the serpent ivering in the bird of prey's beak as he flew off. Dawn found the field mouse at the entrance to usual hole, a spot that, minus obstacles, it uldn't have taken more than half an hour to

clearing out the bumblebees' nest, the field mouse feasts their eggs.

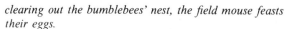

reach. But someone else was there! The bumblebees who had spent the winter in a nearby hollow tree had appropriated his home, apparently deciding that it would be an ideal place to nest and lay their eggs.

This was really too much! The mouse wasted no time. In a flash he stuck his nose in and cleaned out the whole lot—eggs, bees and all their food. Then he simply moved in with his mate, and together they set about raising a large family to help them at least minimize the effects of predation by their natural enemies.

In the process, they once again proved the old country saying that one farmer out of six spends his life working for the rodents.

Will our mouse survive until it is time once again to take up winter quarters in the stable? We can't say; but one thing is sure. If he isn't there himself, one of his relatives certainly will be, gobbling up oats in the manger and elegantly smoothing his whiskers.

Bumblebees' nest

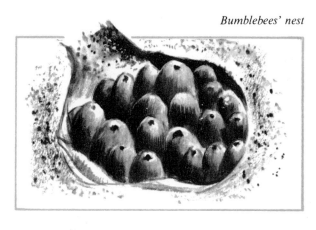

MARCH

The Hare Gets Married

The hare deserves every name that farmers and hunters have ever given him: "Old Buck," "the Friar," "Ginger," "Carrots," "Big Ears," "Old Whiskers." He is a superb animal with a gray-brown coat that's white in front. He has black tips to his long ears and bushy tail.

It is said (but no one can prove it!) that he cannot see straight ahead. It is, in fact, probably true that he sees better at an angle, due to the way his eyes are set in his head, but in any case, the slightest movement draws his attention.

More than once he has had to fight another hare who tried to share his pasture—and his doe!

He eats a bit of everything, depending on the season: wheat when it is ripe, sprouting rye, almost any kind of grass—and he always cuts the stems at an angle about eight inches from the ground. His favorite of all, however, is the wild chicory, or succory, with its beautiful blue flowers.

Like most of the other animals of field and forest (except the migrators, naturally) he never roams too far, preferring the same paths, or runs, and the same feeding grounds.

He also relies as much on his fine sense of smell as on his hearing (though it seems more natural to fully exploit the magnificent ears nature has given him).

Enemies are all around him. Man, of course, tops the list, as hunters have a fondness for fine roasted hare, and there are also dogs, wild cats (or domestic cats who revert to the wild state), wild boars, and other threatening animals.

In any case, this fine evening when the buttercups are in bloom is one particular hare's wedding day. He has several of these annually, of course, but as it's common knowledge that March hares are apt to be a bit mad, and this is the season when the sap is rising, it is definitely an unusual occasion.

Leaving his narrow hiding place under the brambles, he springs forward with ears raised, tail high in the air. Even more alert than usual, he hops along to meet his mate at whatever pace his mood dictates, for there are no pursuers. The doe leaves her own retreat a little later; her ears, unlike his, are flattened down against her body.

Hares are essentially nocturnal animals, feeding at dawn and resting through the rest of the day. However, on rainy evenings (and heaven knows it can rain during March!) they go to their feeding grounds earlier, and they do the same on their wedding days.

The bridegroom has his own territory—a stretch of fields or meadow where he will allow no intruders and where he has his favorite "runs." When he dies, another hare will appropriate this territory and use the same paths, though no one knows just why.

But we are getting away from the subject. This is a wedding day! Off the groom skips through the

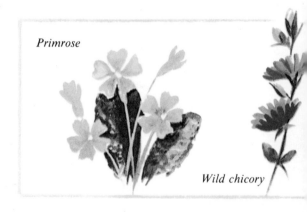

Primrose

Wild chicory

One fine spring evening, Old Long-Ears meets his mate in a sunny clearing.

meadow, cavorting and gamboling before his mate and impressing her no end. Later on, they'll have many babies to take care of, and while our hare may not be the best husband in the world, he is certainly a fond father.

What a fine marriage for early springtime. Yet the ceremony must be rather hurried, for, to tell the truth, the frost is not entirely over, and even though the April flowers will soon be sprouting, hares hate cold, snow and rain.

MARCH

The Tits
Find Nesting Places

All winter long, the tits (close relatives of the Northern American chickadee) have come to peck at the suet strung up on a branch in the garden. First a handsome little blue tit with white head, blue cap and black collar; then the coal tit, greenish except for its yellow breast. As for the marsh tit, it has stayed at home in the woods, as has the long-tailed tit. Nothing seems to escape their notice. Let an insect momentarily lulled by the warm sun begin to try its wings, and presto! it is gobbled up.

The little blue tit brings a caterpillar to its hungry chicks.

Any robin trying to get a share of the suet when a blue or coal tit is hungry is soon driven away to await its turn. Perched on a lilac stem, the robin must watch and wait, its red breast puffed out with excitement.

Two of the blue tits seem more determined than the rest; they're on the lookout for a good nesting place.

The coal tits have the same aim in mind, and their ardor cannot be restrained. In the process of inspecting every tiny crack in the bark for a cocoon or spider, they make a tour of the entire orchard. They too seem compelled to fly to the highest reaches of the mighty ash tree where the male can cry out a triumphant "ti, tipu! ti ti pu!" to one and all as a signal that spring is finally coming. As if the thrush, already nesting, weren't fully aware of the fact!

The blue tits make the most of their cousins' activity to alight on an old plum tree growing next to the house. They have their eyes on a little hole between two stones that was occupied by a couple of wrynecks last year. These former tenants haven't yet returned from their winter sojourn in Africa, and by the time they do arrive the first clutch, or brood, of

little blue tits will have been born. But then, perhaps they won't come back at all, choosing the forest to nest in instead.

After two little hops along a branch, the tits slip into the hole quick as mice. Inside it's dark and smells a bit of rats, but a good cleaning will take care of that.

In a few hours their new home is ready, lined with moss, down, a few feathers and even some wisps of cobweb. The only thing that remains to be done is to fill the nest with a dozen or so little cream-colored eggs, nicely decorated with tiny brown spots.

The coal tits haven't been so lucky. Oh, well, it doesn't really matter. They have decided to go back to their old nest in the apple tree at the bottom of the garden, and they start to repair it immediately.

Let the March winds blow, our winter friends are now safe and snug in their nests.

When the baby blue tits finally leave the nest, they'll have a white-blossomed plum branch to perch on. And there they will be, a dozen balls of fluff crowded against each other, their mouths wide open to welcome the host of insects brought back by their busy parents.

Except for the farm cat, no one will notice them, for all the other birds will be equally busy, singing away as they build their nests for future clutches.

Blue tit

Coal tit

Long-tailed tit

Great tit

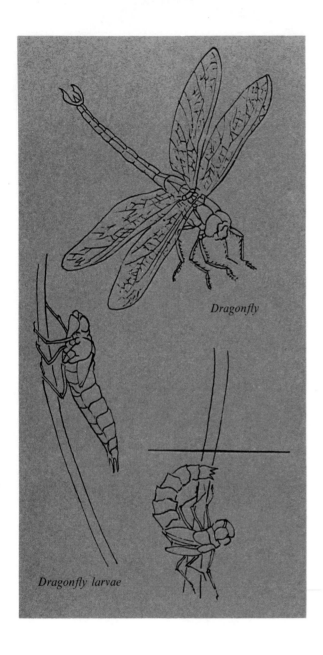

Dragonfly

Dragonfly larvae

On the Red Hills of Quercy

By the time the willow warbler arrived on the scene, the gaily-clad newt, his crest proudly raised, had already been in the pond for almost a month.

How strange for this usually retiring amphibian, who leads such a sheltered life underground and appears at night only to feed, to make the long excursion to the water. And why had the swift-flying bird abandoned the African sun for this wild corner of Quercy in southwestern France?

The answer is simplicity itself. No animal or bird on earth can resist the call of spring, can refuse the instinctive urge to reproduce his kind back where he was born—in his own native land.

Our friend the newt had been born there in the pond, and had lived there as a larva before metamorphosing into a newt. Our lively warbler, on the other hand, had first seen the light of day near the ruins of an old monastery nearby. Both had to obey their instincts and come back.

Yet feeling a bit lonely on this warm March afternoon, the willow warbler flew aimlessly from branch to branch before pausing on a wall to sing a brief tune to his mate. She had already begun to build a ball-shaped nest with a tiny hole on top. Except for their green coats and sunny yellow breasts and shorter beaks, these two might have been taken for garden warblers. All the materials

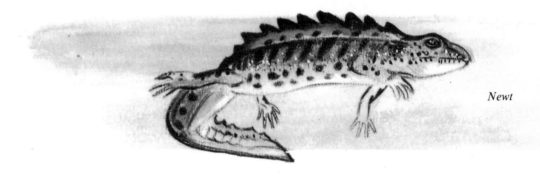

Newt

40

Willow warbler

eeded for their nest were close by: little wads of wool caught by brambles when wandering sheep browsed in the meadow, dried moss, the fluff from thistles, the thousand and one little things it takes to make a proper home. Some little flies revealed their whereabouts underground by buzzing beneath the oaks; and like the tiny spiders running along the edge of the well, they were quickly gobbled up.

But be careful! Overhead a sparrow hawk with pointed wings blazes swiftly through the sky on the lookout for a newt threading his way home along secret paths through the fresh green grass. Or perhaps he has his eye on the larva of a dragon fly just emerged from the pond to rest on a twig before spreading its transparent wings. Anyway, our little willow warbler is safe in the tree which serves as both his refuge and his larder. He certainly deserves his Latin name of *Phylloscopus,* or "leaf inspector,"

for he spends all his time hopping from one leaf to another in search of cocoons, insects and caterpillars. And, naturally, when their clutch of eggs has hatched, the parent warblers will redouble their efforts; by that time there will be swarms of mosquitoes above the pond and plenty of flies.

Early to arrive and early to leave, the willow warblers make the most of their opportunity. They will leave for the south later than their brethren from England, Germany and Scandinavia, but by August, when the blackbirds are fattening up on mulberries, they will have taken off for Africa. On route they will stop to visit some cousins who never leave the south of France, and then they will continue on their long voyage to the sunny climes they love so well, where delicious things grow that keep their stout little hearts beating through the long winter season.

SPRING

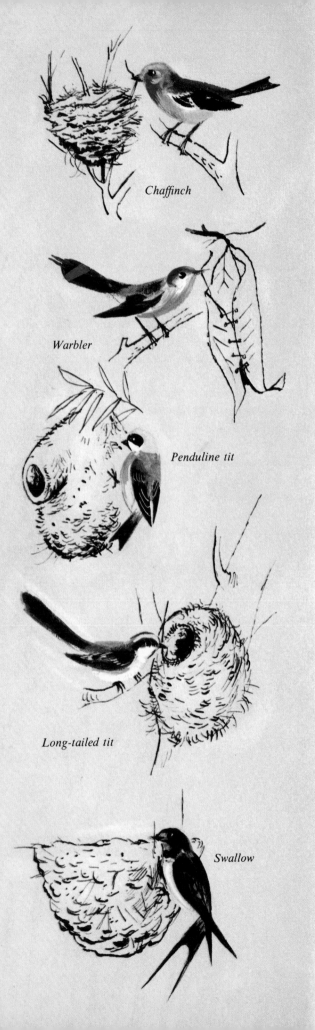

Chaffinch

Warbler

Penduline tit

Long-tailed tit

Swallow

Springtime Architects

Birds took up the building trades long befor
men did, and according to their species, they can b
masons, carpenters, tailors, woodcutters or embank
ment builders.

Trees are the favorite nesting places for mos
songbirds. Finches, for instance, tend to tuck thei
deep and comfortable nests into a tree's mossy forl
lining them with lichen, moss and spider webs.

On the other hand, the tailorbird warbler o
southern Europe chooses a large leaf, punches hole
along its edges and then neatly laces them togethe
with vegetable fiber.

The penduline tit weaves himself a round ne
hung from the outmost branches of a willow tree
Though it swings in the wind, it is well attached an
quite safe from would-be marauders, who are ur
able to venture out onto these fragile twigs.

One of the prettiest nests is built by th
long-tailed tit, who works for many a week to com
plete his pear-shaped dwelling of tightly wove
moss covered with lichen and lined inside with
thousand feathers. Within this charming home, th
mother tit lays tiny white eggs that are speckled wit
pink.

Both swallows and house martins become mason
when nesting time comes around. Moistenin
mouthfuls of earth with saliva, they make a past
which becomes a solid mortar when dry and whic
sticks beautifully to the walls they favor. Little b
little and bit by bit they thus erect a cup which the
then line with feathers for the comfort of thei
scrawny offspring.

Still another mason is the nuthatch; he uses hi
beak as a trowel. He usually builds his nest in a tre

There are as many ways to build a nest as there are species of birds, and each has its own specialty.

crutch, using thin pine slivers covered with clay. Its entrance tends to be narrow indeed.

Woodpeckers, as their name implies, are carpenters rather than masons. With their powerful beaks they hammer out holes large enough to shelter a clutch of white eggs, which usually lie directly on sawdust. It is not unusual to find several woodpecker nests one above another in the same tree, rather like apartment units.

Seen from a distance, a magpie's nest appears to be simply a bundle of thorns. Nevertheless, like the nest of a blackbird or a jay, it has a sturdy foundation on an earthen platform. And the unimpressive bundle of sticks are actually carefully woven together into a sphere, the interior being padded with feathers, dried grass and moss. Thus the magpie is simultaneously a carpenter, roofer, weaver and upholsterer, and his masterpiece weighs almost seven pounds!

Following a long-established family tradition, some water birds construct floating nests, sometimes on open water, sometimes between sheltering reeds.

Certain birds like nutcrackers don't take much trouble with their abodes; these happy-go-lucky types may even choose to simply plop themselves down in a tuft of mistletoe.

Still others, such as the woodcock, lay their eggs on the ground. Although a woodcock nest weighs a mere 6 or 7 ounces, 400 oak and aspen leaves have been used to make it!

Many sea birds make do with a slight indentation in a cliff garnished only with a bit of seaweed. Perhaps they realize that on their almost inaccessible islands they have little to fear except for an occasional renegade sea gull.

Then there are the nest thieves, lazy birds who brazenly take advantage of others' work. Among these are the sparrows who drive swallows from their nests and the bold nutcrackers who sometimes appropriate the homes of squirrels.

Springtime architects are not merely clever craftsmen but true artists as well, for many of them are the accomplished songsters who make gardens so delightful when April comes along.

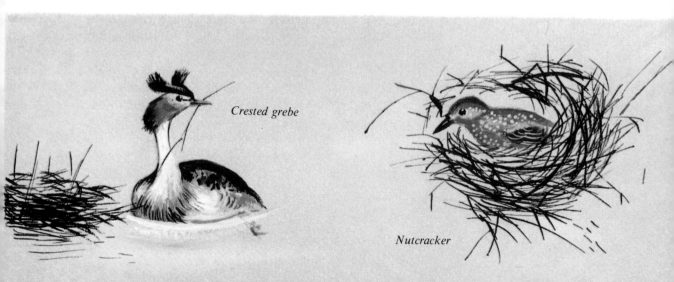

When the Swallows Return

The popular saying has it that one swallow doesn't make a summer—but would spring truly be spring if these feathered speed demons were not seen overhead? With their uncanny homing instinct they can unerringly fly as much as 6,000 miles back to the last year's nest under the eaves of an old barn.

Having reached Portugal in February, they swirl like feathered darts around the village steeples.

There they spend several days, skimming over the heavy-laden orange trees and darting past the ferocious bulls and their followers, the snow-white egrets. For fun? Hardly! Swallows have but one idea in their black and blue-flecked heads—to catch insects and to gobble them down just as fast as possible.

Practically their entire lives are spent on the wing, and a lot of their activity is devoted to satisfying their tremendous appetites. They hunt in flight, they drink and bathe while skimming over the still waters, and they are still on the wing when they pick up bits of mortar here and there with which to patch their nests.

The truth is, they could remain in Portugal, where there is plenty to eat; but age-old instinct impels them to go back to their first home. However, instead of traveling in groups as they do in the fall, the swallows make their spring migrations alone and in short hops.

No matter if the spring equinox tosses the sea, the swallows continue their voyage despite storms and fatigue, in the sky from dawn to dark, gracefully darting and swooping with their mouths ever open in search of food. Sometimes a bird accidentally swallows a bee whose sting kills it seconds later. Others are caught in nets and end up roasted on spits.

But most swallows leave the minarets of Portugal,

One swallow may not make a summer, but his appearance means fine weather is on its way.

its fighting bulls, egrets and perpetually croaking frogs. They soar in the sky as they fly northward, almost lost to sight against huge storm clouds rolling in from the Atlantic.

Dusk finds them in a mountain village, thousands of pointed wings darting above the roofs, and at dark they line up like soldiers on every available telephone wire. All night long they chatter to one another in raucous voices that pierce the air like needles. Singly or in pairs they join in mad flights, tracing arabesques in the sky with ever-open beaks to receive the smallest insect prey.

Through the night, huddled together behind a shutter, they twitter away. And what they say, so softly as to be almost unheard, we will never know. But they will probably be thinking of tomorrow's departure and the nest that awaits them.

By the time the sun has risen again there's nary a swallow to be seen in the village.

And one April evening, before a barn, the sun will shine on a couple of black backs as they busily build their nest. The swallows are home once more.

APRIL

The Masters of the Early Morning

The skylarks which spent the winter in the fields of southern Europe have now once again gone north.

Those who have decided to remain in southern France and in Italy have taken possession of their vast territories. It is said that in the world there are some 80 species of lark, all of whom require a great deal of space. On this April morning, when the tender vine leaves are beginning to form garlands from one post to the next, four fledglings will soon be born in the hollow nest snuggled against a clump of earth.

In March, two males had battled for the affections of a female lark who led them on a merry chase through the grass. The mating period is the only time, in fact, that these birds show the least tendency to be aggressive.

While the female lark patiently broods over her eggs, the male broadcasts his joy to all the world from high above.

Barely has the first pink touched the sky with a new day when the father lark will leave his furrow and take flight.

Singing all the while, he will rise straight toward the blue, soaring so high that he becomes only an invisible voice lost in the sky, his limpid music filtering downward from the clouds to rejoice men's hearts.

Then suddenly, folding his wings to his side, the lark will fall like a stone to alight near his wife and brood hidden in the grass.

Skylarks have jointed toes and outsized nails to help them walk, yet they never perch. The sky and the plains are their domain, where they live their lives, raise their young—and eventually die. Their neutral color serves as camouflage, which is just as well for there are always plenty of people eager to transform them into tasty pies.

After only a few seconds on the ground, our lark takes flight again to release a fresh outburst of song. His mate listens admiringly, head cocked to one side, as she sits on her nest.

Sparrow hawk

Buzzard

Falcon

Twelve days later, four tiny chicks hatch—so minute that a clover leaf could cover each. Noisy and lively, they are also obedient. Their earth color and the fact that they know enough to stay absolutely still frequently saves their lives.

Danger constantly threatens them. Other wings skim over the ripening wheat and circle in the sky—hook-beaked birds of prey: the hawk, the buzzard and the falcon. And the stealthy paws of bloodthirsty little animals tread the ground, their keen noses sniffing out the nests of quails, partridges and larks.

Only three weeks after birth, the young larks are able to take to the sky, and their parents have time to think of a second or perhaps even a third clutch of eggs.

Though the ancient Gauls considered larks sacred and even made them the symbol of their country, Frenchmen today tend to prefer larks in meat pies and are quite willing to kill them off by the hundreds for a few mouthfuls. Fortunately, despite the hunters, there are still enough of these blythe spirits left to fill spring days with song.

APRIL

Springtime
on the Farm

It isn't just because a rooster crows earlier than the winter crow or the summer dove that we count on him to announce the spring. (After all, at times a rooster will even call exultantly to the moon in the middle of the night lest another bird beat him to it!)

In the dark of the hen house, the uncrowned king of the barnyard keeps silent while heavy spring rains beat down upon the tiles.

But comes a fine April morning, and there he stands on the wall, puffing out his chest and raising his saw-toothed crest. His hen lady friends—Leghorns, Sussex and fancy-hatted Houdans—timidly peeking out from under their wings, listen to his rousing call and then run for the feed box.

A large gray hen, the one with a cape, waddles along surrounded by her brood of pink-legged chicks. For it is nesting season on the farm, and latecomers are apt to miss their meals.

The barnyard duck who sat so faithfully on her clutch of eggs for 26 days has already led her downy yellow ducklings to the pond, there to paddle about happily.

And the cows, who spent a dull winter indoors in their stable, have sniffed the clean spring air with their moist black muzzles. They hurry out into the pastures in search of tender green shoots. Accompanied by their unwanted cloud of flies, they ignore the farm's watchdog and press through the gate that leads to the meadow with its hedge of flowering hawthorn.

"Shoo, shoo," cries the herdsman to urge them on, while the dog barks and nips at their heels to keep them in line.

"Cockadoodle doo," cries the rooster in his strident voice, a sure sign that the day has gotten off normally (for, as always, our rooster must have the last word).

The duck teaches its young to swim in the pond

When April comes, the cows are led out to pasture to feed on tender young grass.

Amidst the violets that grow by the hedge, the gray hen and her brood hunt for tiny snails, their feet ever scratching at the little mounds of soft earth that mean there are tender pink worms underneath.

It may be a little early for the farmer's wife to take outside the pots of geraniums which have decorated the kitchen all winter, but she eagerly awaits her first flower; her husband thinks only of watching his grain grow in the fields.

In the evening, the rooster counts his family as they file back into the hen house. The cat, with half-closed eyes, watches the procession smugly, as if to say, "Get on your perch, poor things. Everyone knows you're only chickens."

There is a terrible racket in the hen house as they try to settle down, two hens disputing which has the right to a favorite roosting place, but finally they all fall silent. Even the rooster.

As a matter of fact, he is already asleep, his head tucked under his wing, getting his forty winks before another April dawn comes and he must sound reveille for all the other animals.

The Grass Snake

Pitter-pat, pitter-pat! How pleasant it is to hear raindrops hit the leaves when one is comfortably coiled and has a full stomach!

The grass snake was sleeping snugly in his lair—a fallen willow near a pond—when he was awakened by the sound of wet leaves being stirred. Sensibly, he remained motionless; the sound was made by his mortal enemy the hedgehog. This foe's presence in the woods meant he was trying to root out a morsel for breakfast. Could he be hoping for a green snake with a black-and-white diamond pattern on his back? Not this time, for the hedgehog stopped disturbing the worms under the leaves and went off toward the pond.

The rain has stopped now, and the grass snake decides to leave his lair. But slowly and cautiously, for the woods are full of other enemies. There's the crow, for instance, some of whose eggs the snake had gobbled down the year before.

He looks carefully before leaving his nest, for now is the time for him to shed his skin. This is a tricky task for all snakes, and if our grass snake has so far eluded the sharp beaks after him, it is due mainly to his own prudence.

Now the sun has come out from behind the clouds, and the snake slithers into a carrot field, his favorite basking place, where he'll stay for hours on end watching the green tufts sway in the slightest

The grass snake and the hedgehog

Wild carrot bloom

The crow hates the grass snake, for the snake frequently robs its nest of eggs.

breeze and darting his forked tongue in every direction so as to discover if anything stirs beneath the grass.

Suddenly his round eyes dilate slightly, and since he has no eyelids, the effect is rather startling. He has just noticed a tree frog hopping from one twig to another. Tempted at first to strike out, he hesitates and then changes his mind. He isn't really very hungry right now, and besides, in springtime frogs abound in the fields; there will be other chances.

As evening falls, our snake slips off toward the pond; he doesn't even have to hunt, for along the way a field mouse's nest supplies his dinner. Sliding into the water, he starts across the pond, his head cutting the calm surface like a knife. As he passes, a couple of moorhens rise from their floating nest and a squirrel in a nearby tree sets up a chatter as if to warn the other animals that an egg thief is in the neighborhood. This time, though, our grass snake has a full belly. Refreshed by his bath, he returns to his nest in the hollow log as the soft April rains again begin to fall.

53

Quails in the Grass

Hearing the pleasant chirps of quails in the April fields, farmers are reminded that this is the month to sow their crops—and in a hurry!

The little birds responsible for this sound have just returned from their winter stay in Africa. Although they belong to the same family as chickens, peacocks and turkeys, there's an immense difference in size; you can easily hold a quail in one hand.

Males of the species are not very sociable, and the love calls they send to their mates also serve as threats to any rival suitors to stay out of their chosen territory.

But now let us turn from the male quail, who will soon be going off anyway, and take a look at his plump little wife. All alone she will construct her nest in the tender grass, and alone she will sit over a clutch of brown-speckled eggs. But her courage will be well rewarded when the eggs finally hatch and she is surrounded by a brood of tiny chicks, lively and alert and forever pecking away at the ground in search of insects to eat.

"Cheep! cheep! cheep! cheep!"

In her dark, white-striped hat and her spotted apron, the mother quail sitting on a bramble bush warns her brood of approaching danger and they all lie low. A hawk passes across the sky high overhead and then is gone.

Now that the warm April evenings have come, the orphean warbler sends his clarion call across the countryside, and in the mornings, the lark's bell-like tones fall from the sunlit sky. But Mrs. Quail is always alert, always on the watch for enemies diving down from the heavens or slithering through the grass, and she keeps careful check to see that none of her chicks are missing.

Quails must be constantly on the lookout for men as well as fowl and snakes. Instead of protecting them, men often hunt down quail relentlessly (quail make excellent game). As a matter of fact, one fine morning Mrs. Quail was almost cut down by a

The mother quail has a busy time keeping track of her mischievous offspring. When fall comes, they will all fly off to a warmer climate.

Colorado beetle

Grasshopper

Warbler

mowing machine! Luckily, she escaped into a nearby field of alfalfa. What a close shave *that* was!

Only five weeks after birth, the little quails are as big as their mother, and their appetites have grown at the same pace. Nothing escapes their notice or their eager beaks: crickets, grasshoppers, ants, earthworms and beetles are all gobbled down.

When the cuckoos leave in mid-August, it is time for the quails to gather together for their great migration. They are accompanied by the corncrake, a shy and elusive bird sometimes called the "king of quails."

Quails take off on tiny wings which appear to be only suitable for short flights, yet in a single night they may fly up to 400 miles. Alas, on reaching their destination many are so exhausted that they simply fall to the earth, to be picked up for the asking by African lovers of roast quail. Let us hope that Mrs. Quail is not among them, and that she will return when April comes again.

The Cuckoo

The cuckoos of Europe come from afar. They have flown all the way from southern Africa, up the valley of the Nile and across the Mediterranean Sea.

They arrive in April, when the forest leaves are still pale green, proudly announcing their arrival with the echoing cry of "Cuckoo, cuckoo."

All the other forest birds would be happier without these robbers, who soon begin to look around to see which nests they can take over. Mrs. Cuckoo must really make a thorough survey, for it is not easy to find an already prepared nest into which she can drop her egg. The fact that cuckoo eggs are small in relation to the grown birds makes her task a little easier; the mother cuckoo can even carry an egg in her bill if she needs to.

It remains a mystery how an individual cuckoo selects various foster parents to rear its young, for cuckoos deposit their eggs with 70 different species throughout the world. Wouldn't it be easier simply to build a nest of one's own and then sit on the eggs for a few days instead of watching the comings and goings of so many birds? For it should be remembered that a mother cuckoo only lays one egg in each nest, and must therefore find several unguarded ones to make sure of having a large enough family.

And so to work, watching and waiting for an opportunity. This particular morning there doesn't seem to be any, for all the nests are occupied. But wait!

Isn't that a hawk above, the gray bird with a black-striped breast? As the little warblers rush for cover, the cuckoo instantly takes over their nest, eating an egg that she finds there and then laying one of her own.

The cuckoo's distinctive call rings out through the woods.
Rather than sit on her own eggs, the cuckoo always deposits
them in other birds' nests.

any times the size of his foster parent, the infant cuckoo's
ppetite for insects and caterpillars keeps the poor warbler
usy from dawn until dusk.

Cuckoos know plenty of tricks and keep an
ver-watchful eye. Sometimes, when a hawk or
ther bird of prey eats the foster parents, or when a
est is damaged by a storm and must then be rebuilt
lsewhere, the mother cuckoo will pick up the twice-
bandoned eggs and transfer them to another, safer
ome.

How many nests does a cuckoo visit?

A cuckoo lays up to twenty eggs in a season, and
hile not all of these eggs will hatch, enough do so
at the world never lacks an abundance of these
eculiar birds.

Even the ugly, featherless new-born chicks are
robbers at heart, launching their careers by pushing
their half brothers out of the nest. As for the poor
warblers, stuck with another's offspring, they have
no time left to sing, but must toil night and day to
fill the infant cuckoo's yawning beak with caterpillars and various insects.

Soon the foster parents look like pygmies compared to their adopted offspring, who crush the nest
with their weight. But do the natural parents care a
bit? Not for a moment!

They have spent the entire morning in the pine
woods devouring tent caterpillars, a dish that only
one other bird will touch, the European hoopoe.
Thus, despite their deplorable habits, even cuckoos
are of some use.

MAY

The Golden Bird

The bright golden bird singing from a poplar beside the water's edge looks like a visitor from some exotic jungle.

He arrives when spring has already left its mark on the trees, so that green leaves hide his brilliant plumage. Squirrels hopping from limb to limb on the old oak do not observe his nighttime arrival, and nobody, in fact, knows of his presence until he announces it with his strident cry of "Lor-ioh!"

This marvelous bird, whose golden color is heightened by elegant black stripes on his wings, now sits in the uppermost branches of the tall trees, his surest refuge. Always he returns to his native clearing, and there, with the help of his green-coated mate, builds a suspended nest in the fork of a poplar.

Made of grass, string, reeds and straw, with an interior lining of down fiber and wool, this masterpiece only lacks a few more strands to make it secure enough to swing in the breeze without endan-

Oriole (male)

The noise of the oriole defending her eggs from a scaveng- ing crow can be heard throughout the forest.

gering its clutch of eggs. Just now, though, it contains but one snow-white egg.

Proud of her work, the hen oriole searches for insects among the trees, leaving to the cock the dangerous task of hunting quick-winged grasshoppers near the ground.

Taking advantage of the orioles' absence, a pirate crow swoops down to the suspended nest, cracks the egg within and is just sucking up its contents when the father oriole returns. His red eyes shining wi

golden arrows will be seen darting through the trees, for the babies will receive their quota of cherries along with healthy helpings of insects. And after a hard day's work feeding his family, the father oriole will slip down to the nearby pond, bathe his golden coat and then find a convenient perch on which to dry his feathers in the sun.

And then, in August or September, when summer wanes, our orioles will start off at night on a long flight to Greece or Egypt where the sun is still warm and where, come winter, there are figs and dates, crickets and grasshoppers to feed on.

ger, he bravely flies at the much larger intruder drive him off through the trees. Nor does he hesi- e to attack a buzzard on similar occasions.

The last skirmish, witnessed by some passing jays well as a squirrel who is combing his bushy tail the sun, causes quite a stir in the forest.

Back at the nest, the oriole finds his mate com- tably installed. That evening she will lay another g, and on the following a third. Maybe even a irth will come later. In any case, neither parent ll leave the nest again for a moment, and both ll take turns sitting on the clutch. When the cher- s in the orchard ripen and the young birds hatch,

Jay

59

The Little Foxes in the Springtime Forest

Five little balls of tawny wool supported by short black legs roll and tumble before the fox's den in the forest.

Observing them through half-closed eyes, their mother feels proud of her mischievous brood. What pleasure she takes in watching them scamper and cuff one another, nip at each others' ears and play tug of war for the possession of a rabbit's foot!

May is playtime for many of the animals born in April. Yet games are more than just play for these little foxes, just as it is for puppies chasing sticks, or for kittens running after balls of wool, or even for the baby goat-like chamois sliding about on icy slopes. For these animal games are a way of preparing for the future. When the little foxes pretend to hide and then leap out to seize a stick, they are really learning the hunting craft. As for the kitten romping with a ball, he is busy training the reflexes and the springing ability that he will need to ambush a mouse.

All are strengthening their muscles. Little warblers beating their wings in the trees are practicing

Cross section of a fox's lair

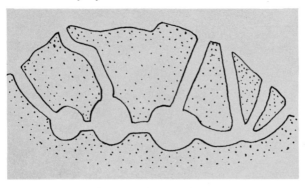

to perfect a speedy retreat from danger, and in the desert baby gazelles practice sudden leaps forward and to one side, their best defense against leopard and lion. Like children, baby animals have their favorite toys—an old bone, a branch or a pebble. Monkeys and bears in the zoo love to play with balls, and it is not always the youngest who have the most fun. How else can we explain the strange behavior of the Alpine raven in his coat of black when he suddenly tumbles and loops all alone in the sky?

The cranes, whose whooping we hear so clearly as they pass overhead, enjoy tossing stones and twigs high in the air and then catching them again in their beaks.

Although mature dogs and cats aren't quite as eager as puppies and kittens, they still love to chase balls even after they have learned their craft. So too, does the lioness on the savannah enjoy playing with her cubs.

Nothing is quite as much fun as watching fox cubs play under the watchful eye of their mother. In the evening when their parents go out hunting, the little foxes will snuggle warmly in their den.

But let us return to our forest. Back from a short hunting trip, father fox snaps his jaws as if to say that the game has lasted quite long enough and there is no point in alerting the enemy. Four little foxes trot Indian file into the den and snuggle close to one another. All we can see in the half light is four little pairs of gray-blue eyes gleaming with mischief.

Outside the fox's den, the forest floor is covered with lily of the valley, the May sun shines down on the new leaves of the trees and only the song of birds breaks the silence.

It is naptime for the fox family.

The Rainy-Day Snail

Two years ago, under a vine root, a little snail was born with a shell so thin and transparent that his tiny heart could be seen beating inside. Yet having spent the next part of his life in the lettuce patch, he now weighs almost an ounce and measures one and a half inches long, quite a respectable size for a snail, even in the province of Burgundy in France.

He has just awakened from his long winter's nap rolled up in his comfortable shell.

As it was only May, no lettuce or strawberries were available, and so, peering through his eyes on the end of their long stalks, he made his way to a quiet corner of the garden where the first tulips were just opening up. Off he moved on his one huge foot, leaving a slippery gray trail on the grass. Born during a thunderstorm, he loved water in any form. But he carefully avoided too-large puddles, for snails have been known to drown in these before reaching the other side. Suddenly he spied a cabbage, a lovely big one all alone in the middle of the garden, its leaves being rapidly shredded to lace by a greedy slug. Ah, he thought, a nice bit of cabbage would make a better breakfast than even the tenderest tulip stem. So he started to climb.

Up, up the curly leaves, our snail was munching away with a will when he suddenly felt himself lifted high into the air by some ruthless force. Peeking out from between two leaves, he couldn't see a thing—but when he was deposited in the rabbit's hutch, that was something else!

Poor snail! He was just a hairbreadth away from being eaten alive by the big gray rabbit, but somehow he managed to crawl down through the wire mesh of the cage and escaped as fast as he could—about 120 yards per hour—back to his native vineyard.

Not a leaf was to be found on the closely pruned roots, but there in the furrows between the rows of vines there was plenty of grass. Once the big pink buds began to appear on the trees, the rest of the countryside was ready to put on its coat of green. Our snail would lead a cautious life, only going out to feed at night. He is a strange creature like no other—with his stomach down near his feet, always carrying his house slightly askew on his back, and with his habit of laying eggs head downward in a hole in the ground.

Always he must watch out for hungry birds and the larvae of glowworms (who can drill through his shell to eat his flesh). When, in midsummer, he sees a tiny greenish light appear in the bushes, he will quickly pull his head back into his shell and stay as still as possible. And when, because of drought, the grass is without even a refreshing touch of morning dew, he will retire to the trunk of a tree and await the long-hoped-for rain.

But what becomes of him in winter? Like man, he will tend to stay indoors, carefully sealing himself in with a film of saliva mixed with lime. And if he has built a double door, beware. It means the winter will be cold.

A snail laying its eggs

A snail's mouth

The snail, born during a thunderstorm, rules over the kitchen garden. Though fond of water, he can easily drown in the shallowest puddle.

His beak wide open, the long-tailed nightjar flies back and forth over the English countryside at twilight. This medium-sized bird is a close relative of the North American nighthawk and whippoorwill.

MAY

Feasting on Air

During the long May evenings a twilight ghost haunts the English skies, skimming through the air to dart among the cows.

Is it true that the nightjar actually takes milk from cows and goats, and does he really deserve the names that farmers call him: "flying toad" and "old goat milker?"

No, not really. And his mother is not a swallow nor his father a toad. He is simply a bird of the twilight, and what he seeks around the herds are dung beetles.

Anyway, how could he nurse with that broad beak slit back all the way to his very eyes? This famous beak of his, which is always wide open as he flies, amounts to nothing more than an insect trap. And one of the best, as anyone can testify who watches him at work.

The june bugs are still up as evening falls, crickets chirp and the downy moths have just left their hiding places. Into the nightjar's sticky mouth they all go! What an appetite he has, and what a wonderf favor he does for us by eliminating so many bother some pests!

Around and around he goes on his springtin flight, this ghostly bird whose hoarse, murmurir cry has startled many an evening stroller.

He flies up to the top of a tree with a noi beating of his wings; the sound resembles that hoofbeats galloping across a plain. Then dov again he floats, as silent-winged as a scops owl the prowl. Tonight, however, our nightjar is worling for his two chicks, hidden away in the unde brush beside a path. Even at their tender age th can hop about in the grass. They have no r nest—only a hollowed out space beneath so ferns—but their mother faithfully sat on the eggs two and a half weeks, leaving them only for a fe seconds at nightfall to stretch her legs a bit.

No sooner do the nestlings leave the nest th another clutch is on its way, and the hardworki

...ightjars build no nests, but ...de under tufts of grass and ...ns.

Nightjar

father has all he can do to keep his growing family in food. How swiftly he flies—but what appetites he has to satisfy! He must work before night falls and then again at dawn before the sun shines over the plain.

But the nightjar is used to this. He sleeps all the day through, perched on a limb or even on the ground, knowing that his bark-colored coat camouflages him completely. Lying quite still while basking in the sun, he is utterly invisible, a real ghost.

As the months drag by, his raucous cry is heard less and less. Then one day he is gone for good. The mad evening flights are a thing of the past. As silently as he came, he goes, accompanied by his mate and a few other nightjars, flying all the way from Lapland to the hospitable plains of East Africa.

65

MAY

The Weasel's Hunt

Rook

Garden spider

It's been raining since dawn. From a snake hole emerges a sharp-snouted head, whiskers bristling. Two tiny mischievous eyes inspect the surrounding territory. Yes, it's still raining; some muddy, dripping rooks are pulling wriggling worms from the ground. The pointed head is followed by a long sandy body ending in a long tapering tail—a weasel. Shaking off the droplets that cling to her fine fur, she seems to hesitate for an instant before reluctantly setting out. Obviously, she has to go: six youngsters wait there under the old elm stump and she must feed in order to be able to nurse them.

Just one of those greedy rooks would have suited her perfectly, but they have already taken flight. She would be equally content to sink her needle-sharp teeth into a tender duckling, but the farm's watchdog is barking from a little distance away. Never mind! She is so sleek, and she knows so well how to thread her way through the nettles in search of food.

Attentive to the least sound, she blinks her eyes, wiggles her velvety ears, rises up on her hind legs and then falls back. Her eyes glisten excitedly; she's decided to raid the farm itself. Off she romps, leaping across a stream in a single bound, stealthily crawling toward a crumbling wall. The less noticeable she is, the better, for her. Despite her small size, she is known to be fierce, with a well-earned reputation for looting the henhouse. But who could possibly smell her under the deluge now pouring down from the heavens? And there on the edge of the path is a little gray gosling, pecking away at the grass with a just-hardened beak.

What a temptation!

The weasel emerges from a pile of rocks, slips across the bottom of a woodpile—and comes face to face with the dog.

The rain had prevented her from scenting his presence. How unfortunate!

But quick as a brown arrow she's off and away, threading through the grass, bounding out of sight. No more weasel. The little gosling was lucky that time!

None of this exactly pleases our friend the weasel, who's now hungrily investigating a spider web that has a grasshopper caught in it. A quick snap of her jaws—phew! Sneezing in disgust she trots off

ward the fields in search of something tasty. At
st! Presto, an egg—presto, no egg. More luck! The
ld mice didn't even know what hit them as she
eaked up from behind. Her hunger satisfied (and
e rain having stopped), she now makes her way to
nearby stream to clean up a bit. She can't stand
ving her fine fur spotted with mud. With a deft
w she wipes her bloody lips, then fastidiously
ans her coat with a pink tongue, washing away
e clots of dirt sticking to her white underbelly.
en she combs her flanks with sharp claws.

After a brief sunbath she starts again for her
me, making a dozen wary detours and pausing

*Returning from a night's hunt at a neighboring farm, the
weasel finds her cubs safe and sound in the old elm stump
where she has hidden them.*

from time to time to rise on her hind legs and have
a look around—as much from sheer curiosity as
from caution.

A final zig-zag around a puddle, one last leap in
the grass and she climbs back into the elm tree
where her little ones wait.

Then zip, there's not a soul in sight. Just a vast,
spectacular rainbow which arches its glorious colors
across the sky.

Ladybird, Ladybird!

A ladybird beetle has spent the night nearby under the clumps of campanula edging the flowe bed. She's a brilliant red bead of an insect whos smooth wing-sheaths form a shell decorated wit tiny black dots.

Now that it's morning, she scurries with lightnin speed on her six legs up the stalks of fresh, ne fennel plants where the little aphids are born.

How innocent she looks, this seven-dotted lady bird! She has even acquired the reputation fo bringing good luck, though to other insects she anything but lucky.

Look at her now, comfortably installed on th stem of a rose bush covered with the little aphid which eat up the buds. A quick movement of he mandibles to the right, then left, and she ha grabbed her prey, ground it up and gobbled down.

The other aphids are quite unaware of any loss i their number and busily continue browsing on wha they consider private territory. For every ten tha are eaten up, another hundred thousand will b born. They reproduce so fast that scientists hav calculated that under ideal breeding conditions, th descendants of a single aphid would soon cover a the continents and weigh more than all mankin put together!

Rather than be smothered in aphids, let our lady bird devour them with a vengeance. Yet even he great appetite is nothing compared to that of he larva, born from an egg laid near the aphid colony This creature is truly terrifying, with a speed on th move which is only matched by its incredible vora ity. The slaughter of aphids will continue for th entire metamorphosis period of about three week

From time to time, ladybirds of other colors an sizes join her in the hunt, as do some handsom

Ladybird beetles have huge appetites for aphids and devo them by the thousands.

coal tit pecks away at the rose bush
search ot tasty aphids.

lden beetles with metallic shells who eat at the
ry heart of the blossoms. One evening one of
ese brazen creatures even knocked our ladybug
 her perch, and she had a tremendous amount of
uble righting herself.

Ladybirds are not the aphids' only enemies. An-
her is the larva of the lacewing, a lovely
le-green insect with transparent wings and eyes
e twin tiny golden pinheads. And then there are
e birds, of course.

Just a moment ago, a busy little tit came to hover
out the rose bushes, chose a twig on which to
rch and then pecked away at random. Our lady-
rd just had time enough to dash between the pet-
s of a newly opened rose. The tit might not have
cked her up, but who knows? Then our ladybird
t drowsy, and decided to rest there near the heart
 the flower bed; she well deserved her nap, this
eful aphid-eater.

Perhaps when autumn comes she will slip unseen
to the house to sleep away the winter months in
e fold of a drape, as the house bugs who lived all
mmer under the trees now scurry from the logs in
e fireplace. But this would be a bad time to chant
e old children's refrain, "Ladybird, ladybird, fly
 ay home . . ."

Let us leave her alone, warm and comfortable
here she is, for when springtime comes again she
 ll once more help rid the roses of their aphids.

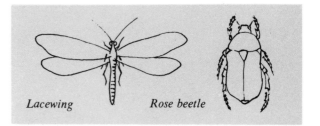

Lacewing   *Rose beetle*

The Shepherd Ants of the Rose Bushes

Among the thousands of ant species in the world the most familiar to us are neither hunters nor warriors. Nor do they fill granaries with grain. They are simply shepherds in the rose garden, a lovely sounding title for the ants that herd aphids. This no mean achievement, but fortunately these slim-waisted ants possess powerful mandibles, or jaws, that can drill, bite and saw, and are used protect the aphid herds from their enemies. Furthermore, they have still another weapon—an evil smelling, caustic liquid which they can spray at will

None of their fighting talents are being brought into play on this pleasant June morning. We see an ant going from aphid to aphid with a solicitude that would be touching were it not for the fact that ant always have some sensible ulterior motive. In this case, the ant is "milking" its herd of aphids. One of the latter has its sucker deep in a rose bud, drawing out sap, and beside him the patient ant-shepherd pats it on the back as if to say: "Well done, it time to give me some milk." No sooner said than done. As the tiny insect continues to drink, he simultaneously gives up his surplus, a little sticky drop instantly lapped up by the ant. Going from aphid to aphid the ant is soon puffed out to alarming proportions. Then he takes his bloated self back to the

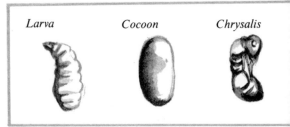

| Larva | Cocoon | Chrysalis |

members of the colony having different tasks: for instance, some care for the young, some guard against enemies, and some collect food.

All morning long, endless lines of ants thread their way back and forth from the ant hill to the roses. Should a few grains of dust fall on their antennae they immediately brush them clean, for these are the delicate instruments they use for telling direction and smelling.

If the weather becomes uncomfortably warm, the ant will lead his herd into the shade under the leaves. Good heavens, there's a red ant! What is he doing here? How can this eater of dead butterflies and beetle shells dare trespass here?

But suddenly everyone, including the red ant, dives for cover: two blue tits flutter down into the rose bushes, land on a twig and then go after every insect in sight. Had they stayed a minute longer, our ants would have disappeared down one of their gullets.

Luckily, a shot aimed at some sparrows that are ravaging the cherry trees scares the tits off as well, and once again the garden is calm. The roses open their petals to stir gently in the breeze, our ant herds his aphids to new pastures under the leaves, then exchanges greetings with another ant wildly waving its antennae.

Later on in the season, the ant will bury some aphid larvae underground, and next year new-born flies will take their turn sucking sap in the rose garden meadow.

But that time has not yet come, and in the ant's orderly world, each day means a day's work well done.

t hill where guards tap and feel him to make sure is swollen creature really belongs to the colony. hen he doles out his store of nourishment mouth to outh.

These ants, like all other ants, are social insects. hey live and work together in groups, with various

Black ant   *Red ant*

An ant herding aphids

June on the Island of Corsica

Unlike many of this Mediterranean island's famous bandits, the little mouflon (a species of wild sheep) didn't take to the hills in order to hide; he'd been born there on the mountainside when the violets were in bloom.

In only three months he had become a rugged little beast, climbing, jumping and cavorting on the rocks, a little hard-headed by nature perhaps, but independent, too.

His bad-tempered mother watched him constantly, bleating imperiously when he tended to wander off or play the fool in some other way. Caution was a necessity, for otherwise there would soon be [...] herds of wild sheep left up on the heath. Our lit[...] mouflon would understand this eventually, but rig[...] now he was intent on climbing as high as he cou[...] to join his father at the top of the cliff. From t[...] vantage point they would look calmly down into t[...] dizzying chasms where lovely springtime torren[...] bubbled and cascaded before drying up complete[...] in summer.

Like other mouflons, he would in time learn [...] do without, to carry on even when thirsty, for [...] summer the blazing Corsican sun withers the tou[...] grass, burns the leaves of the trees to a metal[...] hardness and cooks the green of the stunted bush[...] so that only prickly thorns are left.

This fine June day, however, instead of climbi[...] to the peaks as usual, our little mouflon has decid[...] to explore the chestnut forests. He wants to take [...] closer look at the half-wild pigs that root among t[...] ferns in the forest floor. He already knew the wi[...] goats, having encountered some of these slight[...] mad, acrobatic climbers during his excursions [...]

The little Corsican mouflon comes down from the heights to watch the half-wild pigs rooting about among the ferns under the chestnut trees.

the mountainside, little kids who jumped with their feet neatly held together over the clumps of low-growing shrubs. And from a distance, his keen eyes had also seen little donkeys nibbling the thistles and waving their long ears.

They too live a rugged life, feeding on whatever they can find in this barren land.

Jumping from rock to rock as he cavorts down the mountainside, our little mouflon amuses himself by setting off miniature avalanches. Now and then he stops to sample tufts of grass that seem slightly more tender than those growing on the peaks above. An evening breeze stirs the leaves of the scrub oaks and makes patterns in the tall grass. At last he reaches the chestnut trees. How beautiful they are with their leaves spread out like green hands! However, he is unused to large trees, being raised where the trees are twisted and stunted, and the forest darkness makes him ill at ease. Instinctively he stands still, waiting.

Suddenly the ferns below him part to reveal a huge, black, grunting creature followed by eight squealing piglets. Behind, he notices the gleaming eyes and long white tusks of their father, and sheer terror impels him to run away faster than his limber legs have ever carried him before.

It is truly wonderful how fast he climbs, upward over the fallen rocks and through the gullies, ever upward to finally disappear behind a ridge.

The shadows are already lengthening; it is getting late. Before the wild cyclamen flower covers the land with its purple carpet, the little mouflon will have forgotten his escapade. He'll have matured a bit more, and become cautious and sensible. When snow forces the wild boar to uproot the heather and to sleep huddled close to one another for warmth in their den amidst the ferns, our little sheep will take shelter under an overhanging rock, sharing it with his fellows according to the custom of all other wild sheep, whether in Corsica or elsewhere.

73

The Nightingale's Song

We first heard the nightingale's song just after th cuckoos arrived.

It was just a voice coming from a low-hangin branch by the side of the road. A momentary paus perhaps, before he flew off toward the north or ju: to a nearby clearing.

The nightingale loves thickets, scrub pine an low-hanging branches. Once home, he sings da and night to let the world know that he's taken po: session of his territory and to invite his mate to joi him there, to let her know that he is waiting fc her.

On May and June evenings while his mate sits o her eggs, and no other sound disturbs the stillnes he raises his quivering throat to the sky, releasin his incomparable song for the world to hear. N longer does he sing during the daytime, but fror twilight until dawn enchants whoever listens. First soft flutelike note which he repeats and holds, an which then rises to a crescendo—a song no othe bird can imitate. Never is his song quite the sam becoming more beautiful as night progresses.

A ray of moonlight reveals our virtuoso, a insignificant-looking sparrowlike bird wearing coat of nondescript brown, barely six inches lon and weighing less than half an ounce. Yet through out the spring a marvelous voice comes from th slim body—a voice so strong it can be heard half mile away.

Other songbirds awaken the countryside wit their songs: the lark in the middle of the night an the finch from 3 o'clock on. They are followed b the robin and by the warbler, which sings a sof murmuring melody almost as if it were talking t itself.

As the springtime evening falls, the nightingale raises h throat to the sky and sings his beautiful song.

Yet the voice no other bird can aspire to, the voice which has inspired poets and musicians for ages past, belongs only to the nightingale.

It is said that he sings because he is happy, that he sings because the lily of the valley is in bloom, or because flowers have raised their heads in the ditches. Actually, however, he is singing for an entirely different reason.

his nest near the ground, sheltered from the rain but not too safe from marauders and thieves. He can't be sure that a shrike won't manage to carry off a baby nightingale to its larder in the thicket, or that a passing jay won't whisk one away. Even a tit is not above committing some fearful crime.

Tail spread and puffed with pride, the nightingale hops from bush to bush, gathering insects and

Chaffinch   *Warbler*

Nightingale (female)   *Shrike*

The nightingale sings because, hidden away in the underbrush, his mate is sitting on a precious clutch of eggs.

And it is true that once these eggs have hatched, the nightingale stops singing. From being the golden voiced enchanter of the forest, he turns into a businesslike and watchful bird. For he has placed

worms, and as the warbler in the treetop above murmurs his soft song, he utters a sharp, angry cry at the approach of any intruder.

At the end of summer, he will depart for warmer climes, but when the April cuckoo comes again he'll be followed by the nightingale, and once more the woods will ring to his lovely voice.

JUNE

From the Vegetable Garden to the Stream

For three days now, the little turtle in his box had been on a hunger strike. He had just arrived from North Africa, and, on the pet shop's recommendation, was being offered tender little snails and juicy slugs. But he refused them all. In desperation we gave him a dandelion flower, and he immediately set to with a will.

Then, when we freed him from his box, he wandered out into the vegetable garden and there, away from prying eyes, had himself a feast among the rows of lettuce and strawberry plants.

How old do you suppose he could be? Hard to tell. When newly hatched, he weighed no more than a fraction of an ounce, and now that he is almost six inches long, he must be around ten years old. Like all other reptiles, he will continue to grow throughout his life, though not so fast as formerly,

and the black spots on his shell will become smaller. But we will probably never know exactly how long he lives.

After a few days, he decided to leave for the forest, perhaps because he was attracted there by the scent of mushrooms, or simply because he wanted to be free. That June we only saw him one other evening, as he nibbled at the stem of a mushroom.

He would probably not return, when the first winter rains fell, to dig a nest in the compost pile at the bottom of the garden, choosing instead to bury himself in dead leaves on the forest floor.

Did you know that Europe's largest reptile is a turtle—the box turtle whose shell measures almost 8 inches? (Another reptile, the ringed grass snake, may grow to be 6 feet long—but it is still not so *large*.) The box turtle has his shell firmly anchored to his

pine, and, like all reptiles, he is a cold-blooded animal.

Ours now lives comfortably on the banks of a nearby stream, but a great deal of patience is required to find him as he lies basking in the sun on a stone; the least sound sends him diving for the bottom, and his hearing is exceedingly sharp. And once down, it will be some time before his dark yellow-spotted head reappears again. For five whole years, from the time he was born in a nest scratched by his mother's claws, his main business was just to stay alive. Barely an inch long, imagine what easy prey he was for snakes and rapacious birds. Now, thanks to his sturdy shell, there is little for him to fear.

Moving from a temperature of 50°F in the water to 104°F in the sun doesn't bother him. He loves to lie on a burning stone, digesting his lunch, before diving into the stream to cool off.

And no longer does he thrive on dandelion flowers. He disdains these as well as watercress,

1 *Box turtle*   3 *Turtle skeleton*
2 *Common turtle*   4 *Grass snake*

unless there is a tender snail hidden under a leaf. Nothing can resist his powerful hooked beak. So much the better for our garden vegetables! He eats minnows, too, the tiny bits of silver shimmering in the pools under the willows in the dappled sunlight. Whether the fishermen like it or not, some minnows won't grow up to fill their pans!

Did you know that the largest reptile in Europe is a turtle?

The Proud King of the Zoo

Towering chesnut trees spread their leafy mantl over the zoo, and on this fine June afternoon, spar rows and starlings hop about on the sun-dapple lawns.

From time to time, a pigeon drops down for brief bath in a puddle before flying off, its head an throat glistening with iridescent greens and blues.

Suddenly a hideous, hoarse cry pierces th stillness—"Eon! Eon! Eon!"

A blackbird dozing under a magnolia bus awakes with a start. Make way for the peacock!

The gorgeous bird advances majestically, arrogar and superb, dragging his long tail splattered wit gold. His feather-crowned triangular head elegantl tops a long slim neck of that rare bright blue foun only on a few exotic butterflies.

"Eon, Eon," he cries, and at the sound of hi strident voice, a drab peahen hungrily pecking at th ground like a common chicken leaves her meal t glance in her master's direction. Her coat is undistin guished, and her only aristocratic touch is the roya crown she too is allowed to wear.

In a nearby aviary, safe from marauding alle cats, a second royal spouse broods over her eggs.

A gardener raking the gravel paths pauses in hi work to admire the spectacle of a peacock treatin; his mate to a show. Now the peacock slowly spread his many-eyed tail, prancing and turning to displa it with repeated shakes that make it shimmer.

But the peahen is not very impressed.

She has been watching all this since April, an while her mate continues to turn, revealing an intri cate network of strong quills and sand-colore feathers, she distractedly goes back to pecking a the delicious seeds found here and there in th grass.

Finally the splendid wheel of fire stops its shim mering to be gently folded back in place. Havin hown his fan to the commoners, the King can now return to more mundane matters. After all, like his relatives the turkey and the guinea hen, he too has a belly to fill. Enough of these royal airs and graces! To the feeding trough!

In another nearby enclosure, a third peahen ushers her brood of chicks to their meal. She keeps them well out of the way of their father, for he has an imperious temper and occasionally chastises his offspring with severe pecks on the head.

Mother hen will teach the chicks to roost despite the fact that the zoo is well guarded and far from the Indian forests where their ancestors once roamed. For although no tigers are near, even a common cat can be dangerous.

It is said that peafowl were introduced to Europe in the days of Alexander the Great, and for many years they were served (with all their feathers) at royal banquets. Today, they are simply admired for their beauty, and are the crown jewel of public parks and zoos. No matter if they make bad fathers and are as stupid as chickens, no matter if they are unloving and unloved, they can still enchant us all —provided we cover our ears.

The peacock spreads his magnificent tail just to please his royal harem.

SUMMER

JULY

The Dragonfly and the Earwig

When the yellow swamp iris start to bloom, the little blue dragonfly emerges from the water and from its larva shell and at once starts to hunt the small biting flies called midges. What a marvelous creature the dragonfly is with its delicate body and shining wings, gaily flitting about and barely resting for a second on the tip of a reed. Yet, even in its gadding, it must take care, for there is always the bladder wort, a carnivorous plant which floats on the water's surface and is ever ready to snap up a curious or unwary insect.

A still greater peril, however, comes from the sky: not only from the birds, but also from the little creature's own cousin, the great dragonfly, a brilliant red monster with transparent wings whose zigzag flight resembles that of a swallow and whose loud buzzing can be heard from afar. This fierce hunter seizes everything in its path, from the whirligig beetle skating along the pond's surface to the vine cricket with its sabrelike tail (which is usually enough to frighten off anything but the great dragonfly!). And, of course, it gobbles down little blue dragonflies by the dozen.

In July when the blazing sun seems to fade even the blueness of the sky, and when it actually does evaporate the water from pond and stream, the plants begin to droop and the reeds turn yellow; soon they will be burnt to make way for a new green crop. Dragonflies will continue to hunt the innumerable flies swarming about and to suck a few sugared drops of sap through hollow trunks. And there will be clouds of mosquitoes as well. It is even said that in southern France the great dragonflies dare to attack the cicadas whose strident cries fill the pine groves from dawn to dusk.

Toward the end of July, our little dragonfly will follow a rivulet until it dries up under a willow tree. He is very weary from having experienced so many battles, seen so many of his brothers devoured by other dragonflies of green, white, red and blue, and struggled so many times to avoid being eaten himself.

Then, as the dragonfly folds its wings, it will be time for the appearance of the earwig (who, regardless of hearsay, has nothing to do with anyone's ears!). With its yellow legs, ant head and narrow body the color of old leather, the earwig will suddenly emerged from its nest under a dead leaf.

Unlike almost all other insects, which abandon their eggs and are unaware of their offspring, the earwig lays eggs, broods over its larvae and even protects the young after they hatch.

The dragonfly watches respectfully as the earwig scampers away, being a trifle in awe of this poisonous, long-legged yellow centipede.

Next morning it will be the dragonfly's turn to lay its eggs, a cluster of tiny droplets which it will deposit carefully in an arc on a water-lily pad and then completely forget.

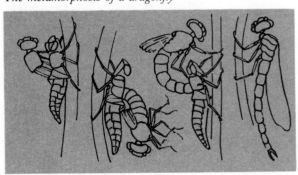

The metamorphosis of a dragonfly

1 Whirligig beetles
2 Vine cricket
3 Earwig
4 Cicada

The Cricket Knight

The cricket in his suit of armor emerged one day from a bright yellow egg placed deep underground. Not unnaturally, he closely resembled his distant ancestors. Long ago he had four or five brothers, all, like him, clad in black armor, but by now only two or three are left to scamper like imps through the tall grass in the meadow. For the meadow is such a dangerous place!

The careful way this little creature sweeps his doorstep and hops to and fro, there can be no doubt that he finds life interesting. When hunger attacks, he grinds up tiny bits of vegetable matter, leaving a trail of infinitesimal holes behind him in the grass.

Happy to be alive, the field cricket chirps merrily by his front door.

*The dung
beetle in his den*

He had a narrow escape while courting, fighting
ith a rival cricket over his bride. Among them-
lves, crickets tend not only to bite and scratch, but
 kick! Worse still, on his honeymoon he ran an
en greater risk—lady crickets have the nasty habit
 eating their husbands whenever possible. Only
s quick wits and nimble legs saved him that time,
d he will certainly think twice before he plays the
dle for a lady-love again.

Indeed, danger lurks everywhere for our cricket.
uring his brief year of life, he must change his
mor ten times or stifle (and each time eat what he
s sloughed off). How awful it must be to feel
mpletely defenseless—body soft, and unable to
read one's russet wings. So far, he has gotten
ong fairly well, spending his days fiddling before
s house, a narrow chamber with a 2-inch tunnel
ening southward toward the friendly sun. Rub-
ng his wings and using his legs as a bow, his stri-
nt song sails forth across the burning summer
ndscape.

Despite the grasshoppers rustling through the
ass and the incessant buzzing of the flies, nothing
owns the piercing notes of our little musician.
nd how well he knows how to modulate his tune,
most as if he were inviting children playing on the
wn to look for him.

And hard to find he is, for he only cuts his little
nfetti in the grass at dawn and twilight, and only
en can we see his round head emerge from his
ir, his antennae quivering.

From time to time, a dung beetle goes by. This
untry garbage collector patiently moistens and
mixes a dung paste before rolling it into a ball to
push home for later use. The dung beetle himself
was born in such a ball of dung, which simultaneously served as nursery and granary, and which
he had to eat his way through before changing into
a pupa and later on into a full-fledged insect. Occasionally, dung beetles will even envelop and bury
such relatively gigantic prey as a dead mouse, storing
him away for future feasting.

Even when birds droop their wings in the shade
of the great trees, the little cricket's song goes on.
And when the thunderstorms that mark midsummer
come, the cricket is quite safe, for he prudently
builds his tunnel on a slope so that it never floods.
Let gypsies sleep under the stars. Our armored
muscian is snug at home.

Crickets only rarely spread their wings.

Ja

Bathtime for the Jay

Yes, it was an ideal time and place for a bath, the jay concluded one warm July evening as he surveyed the cool pool just off a little sand beach that was well sheltered from the sun. He was hot and thirsty, and his wilting feathers needed a good soaking to regain their sheen and flexibility.

Plunging in, he splashed water happily in ever direction as he cleaned himself. Normally so war he almost forgot where he was, though experienc had taught him that with his feathers wet h couldn't make as a quick a get-away as usual i case of danger. Never mind! This secluded sprin

Tits

was well hidden from prying eyes, and only frequented by fellow bathers like himself—the birds. It was a bathtub cut to their size, and the water barely reached the knees of the smallest warbler.

Like humans, birds like to freshen up and cool off, but bathing arrangements are not always as simple as they might be. For instance, goldfinches, tits and starlings prefer to bathe in groups, while others such as jays like privacy.

Soaked to the skin and his crest uncombed, but happy withal, the jay flew to a neighboring branch where he smoothed the feathers of his blue-striped wings and watched the other birds arrive in turn.

Almost immediately a battle broke out. Perfectly willing though the tits were to share the bath with one another, they resented the intrusion of any other species. Feathers puffed out and beaks wide open, they appeared ready and eager to fight for their right to bathe in peace.

Robin

Blackbird

On a nearby bramble bush sat a robin, a peaceful bird prepared to await his turn patiently. And when the tits had departed (appearing half their normal diminutive size), he leapt down onto a floating twig, sank into the water up to his fat round belly and floated there absolutely still, neither splashing nor drinking. He wasn't thirsty, apparently. Like a mirror, the still waters reflected the color of his pretty red breast.

The tranquility didn't last long, however, for now came the blackbird's turn. Imperturbably the jay took in the scene, for as the official watchman of the woods he understood the customs of each clan (a knowledge that enabled him to rob many a nest). He knew very well that the yellow-billed widgeon had to be completely alone, as did the bullfinch, for that matter.

The jaunty jay stationed himself at the forest's edge on a favorite oak where he could nibble at the acorns. Looking out over the surrounding countryside, he could instantly make the distinction between a harmless hiker and a death-dealing hunter. Now he shrieked with alarm as he spotted a falcon's knife-edged wings cut across the sky.

Tomorrow, from daybreak on, the bathers will return one by one to drink the life-sustaining water and, as usual, the jay will watch from his tree. In the evening he will join the group to comment on the day's happenings in his raucous voice.

Kingfisher

JULY

The Beaver's Voyage

A burning July sun beats down through the poplars beside the stream, and the kingfisher on his low-lying branch idly watches fish snapping at flies below.

It is hot, and the beavers are asleep.

In the evening, the bird skims along the surface of the water, singing his soft cricket's cry. He doesn't know—nor would he care if he did know—that this is a red-letter day for two members of the beaver colony, for they are leaving it forever.

Two sleek brown heads cut the surface of the water, leaving a foaming V-shaped wake behind. One beaver slows down after a while and, folding his forepaws to his chest, uses his broad, webbed hind-paws to tread water. His slower brother soon catches up; then, together, they set off toward a new life.

For the past two years, they have learned everything that a beaver worthy of the name must know: how to fell a tree by gnawing it in just the right way, how to trim off its branches and carefully peel them, as well as how to store winter provisions in the depths of their lair. Except in Scandinavia, European beavers don't build lodges; they are no longer safe, for hunters have been tracking beavers down for centuries now. Instead, these industrious animals dig dens in banks, streams and lakes. And yet no matter where they live, water and wood remain the essentials of life to them.

Among other things, these two young beavers know how to make dikes and dams, how to choose the most succulent roots from water plants and how to wash and comb their fur with their agile fore-paws. A beaver's tail is a far more useful instrument than the bushy tail of a squirrel; it is a broad scale-covered appendage which helps him swim and which he can slap against the water with a bang when the slightest danger approaches.

Leaving the stream for the woods, the beavers progress more hesitantly; now they must search for their own food, far from their parents' comforting gaze.

Their choice falls on a young poplar tree, and standing up on their strong back legs, supported by their tails, they saw away with their huge yellow incisors to cut the tree to the ground. What a delicious dinner, and what tender bark! Occupied with their meal, the two beavers don't notice the mill nearby, but they soon set off again. It isn't long, however, before the sound of the barking miller's dog makes them jump into the stream, only rising to the surface again a hundred yards downstream.

As night falls they begin to feel tired, so they hollow out a space beneath a willow and, hugging each other for warmth, settle down for the night.

A beaver's lodge

Later on, they will establish a home on the banks of the majestic Rhone River in southern France and secretly raise families of their own. To beavers, secrecy is always essential, for without it the species could not survive. French kings since the time of the Franks hunted down beavers both for their furs and their musk, and legend has it that certain monks once made sausage out of beaver meat!

Yet the kingfisher will watch them idly as they waddle through the grass. After all, on the banks of the Rhone everyone minds his own business.

With his long, sharp teeth, the beaver can cut through a young aspen and make it fall wherever he chooses.

The Butterfly Kings

During May when the lily of the valley covers the forest floors, and the thrush's song has been replaced by the still finer voice of the nightingale, only a few butterflies were to be seen, among them the cabbage butterfly and the sulphur. Now that it is July, however, the butterflies are kings, for this is the month when most of them lead their brief but beautiful lives.

Like a marvelous red-sailed boat, the copper only comes to rest long enough to taste a flower. The swallowtail prefers pink flowers, while the soufre butterfly enjoys himself most in fields of alfalfa. In the mountains, the common blue dances above the honeysuckle and the mourning cloak likes to extend his long sucker into the hearts of scabious blossoms. The beautiful apollo, transparent wings dotted with red patches, settles on a thistle whenever the sun goes behind a cloud.

Whether they are daytime butterflies with little hammers on the end of their antennae or night-flying moths whose antennae are feathery, each species has its own way of flying and settling down, its own preference for flowers and a favorite time of day. (There are exceptions to this rule, of course; some flowers attract all kinds of butterflies.)

Butterflies like sunshine, appearing in greater numbers during good weather and seeking shelter under leaves at the first sign of a shower. The great sphinx family of moths, on the other hand, never show themselves before dusk, and as a rule their somber coloring makes them hard to see (though even in this family there are brilliant exceptions such as the green sphinx which favors oleander bushes and the pink sphinx commonly found in vineyards). Sometimes the patterns on the wings of these night-flying insects seem designed for de-

Copper argus

Sphinx moth

Cabbage butterfly

Orange skipperling

Argus

Red admiral

Swallowtail

Little tortoiseshell

...main blue

which eventually emerge will eat only leaves from these same bushes.

But there are exceptions to this rule as well, and the common cabbage butterfly illustrates this. It will eat celery, daisies and, naturally enough, cabbage leaves.

Many moths lay their eggs on oak, willow and poplar trees, or even in lichen, while others choose

grasses or low-lying shrubs. And on a really hot day, it is not unusual to see whole swarms of Lycaenidae blues cooling off near ponds and streams.

Only the velvety, dark-winged grayling, as far as anyone knows, lays her eggs as the mood strikes her, dropping them here and there in mid-flight.

The little caterpillars hatched in the meadows crawl up the tall stalks to eat the leaves at night; when dawn comes, they crawl back down again and hide near the roots, well sheltered from the inquisitive eyes of avid insect-eating birds.

...nsive purposes, and the wings of a death's head ...hinx are indeed quite frightening.

All butterflies have four wings, six legs and a ...cker with which to sip nectar from the flowers. ...heir brilliant coloring depends on microscopically ...nall, hollow scales which fit together like tiles on a ...of. They are so delicate that the least touch will ...umble them into dust, revealing the transparent ...bric of the wing below.

As everyone knows, before they become butter-...es, these insects have first been caterpillars and ...en chrysalids.

Just as the butterflies have their favorite flowers, ...o the caterpillar during its lifespan will limit its ...raging to a single species of plant. Europe's largest ...tterfly, *Charaxes jasius,* which loves the summer ...n and feeds on ripened figs, lays its golden eggs ...ly on the leaves of one bush, and the caterpillars

Half-black butterfly

AUGUST

The Mantis
and the Scorpion

Two enemies confront one another in the dry, withered grass, two summer huntresses on a brief encounter: a praying mantis and a poisonous scorpion.

They don't bear much resemblance to each other. One has a long, thin body, twiglike and bright green, quite innocent-appearing with her forelegs clasped together in prayer. A closer look, however, reveals the cruelty of the frightening eyes in her triangular head, and indeed she is the only insect whose eyes can swivel from one side to another like a human's.

As for the scorpion, she has resembled no one else but herself since prehistoric times, millions of years before men appeared on the surface of the earth. She is quite hideous, with her head affixed to her thorax and her mouth on her stomach. Only her small size prevents us from fleeing at the sight of her.

A living nightmare for grassland inhabitants, the mantis preys on crickets. Standing erect on her stilt-like legs and barely moving her saw-toothed forelegs, she is perfectly camouflaged within the greenery.

Her enemy the scorpion hasn't the same appetite, being able to fast for days. She knows, too, that sooner or later, without having to budge, some sort of prey will pass within range of her claws.

Yes, these two are fearsome indeed. Who would imagine, seeing the scorpion dancing with her hu

The praying mantis and the scorpion are each other's worst enemies.

nd and clasping him with her claws, that she
uld devour him once the honeymoon was over?
d the mantis will do the same, gleefully nibbling
ay on her mate's severed head.

On this particular evening the mantis, fleeing
m a bird, had dropped down before the scor-
on's hole, where the latter stood waving the poi-
ned stinger in her tail. Although the mantis wasn't
mpletely defenseless, even her agile claws, which
uld rip apart a grasshopper, were rather
effective against the scorpion's armor and poi-
ned dagger.

Furthermore, she was weighted down by the eggs
her belly. She had been about to deposit them on
tuft of rosemary when the bird almost put an end
her existence. A clumsy flier at best, she now
ed to retreat on her long, stiltlike legs. Would she
ve time to spread her wings? She knew that a set
ttle with the scorpion would be fatal for her: the

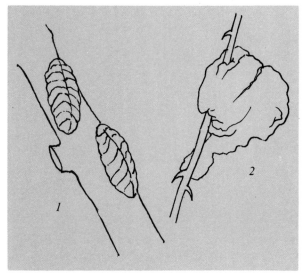

1 Egg cluster of brown mantis
2 Egg cluster of praying mantis

enemy would hold her at arm's length with those
pincerlike claws until the moment seemed ripe to
finish her off.

But the scorpion didn't attack. Perhaps she was
thinking of the day that a wolf spider had spared
two of the transparent offspring who had fallen off
her back, despite a talent like her own for fatally
stinging and poisoning. Actually, the reason was quite
different. Fortunately, she wasn't hungry, being at
that moment engaged in the process of tearing apart
the head of a moth.

Under her evil gaze, the mantis hurriedly spread
her long wings and flew away to the rosemary bush,
there to regain enough composure to lay a load of
eggs.

In a few day, her clutch of eggs could be seen, a
foamlike yellow cluster that is known in southern
France as *tigno,* and which, if gathered at night
under a rising moon, is thought to be a sure cure
for chilblains and toothaches.

Wolf spider

93

AUGUST

The Thirsty Season

August is the thirsty month, the time when water sprinklers are out, when tomatoes on the vine turn bright red and eggplants deep purple. It is also a time when wood wasps buzz about the peach and plum trees.

Flowers shimmer under the burning sun: petunias in all their velvet glory, geraniums, sage and dahlias in their striped extravagance. And the birds seem less noisy than usual.

The little flycatcher, who had followed the golden plover from its northern nesting grounds, now halts for an instant on a fruit-laden fig tree—a brief respite on its long road south.

A few red leaves drift lazily down from the linde trees and the pines shed their needles, the peak of summer now being past. As the heat become stifling and thundershowers growl in the distance signaling the turn of the season, the first swallow sit like beads on telephone wires awaiting the signal to start on their long journey to warmer clime Many another bird will come and go throughout the months of September and October, flying dow from the north where the mulberries have turned a flaming red. Chattering swallows will carefull preen their feathers, fly off to hunt, return to cha once more, and then suddenly, one evening, the will be gone. The next morning there will be hur dreds more, and like the martins who once hovered about the eaves and now have long disappeared they too will vanish.

Bees, little realizing an enemy hovers above, bus themselves about the wide-open flowers that seen so ready to give up their sweet nectar. The hone

By August, when the bees are still sucking nectar from th flowers, some of the birds have left.

94

Wood wasp

must seem to the tiny ant who nonetheless crawls bravely out on a limb, attracted by the sugary yellow drops oozing from its fruit. And that little puddle formed by drips from the lawn sprinkler—how impossibly wide it must appear to the unfortunate aphid that attempts to cross it and finally drowns.

We are grateful for the blackbirds, hedgehogs, carabus beetles and agile lizards who feast on insects. And we should certainly appreciate the owl who hunts fruit-destroying dormice and voles, for with-

...zzard, hungry for these appetizing morsels, dives ...ddenly to seize a dozen at a time; he disdains all ...e less delectable insects, such as the hairy caterpil-...s and the daddy long legs (harvest spiders) who ...arry off as fast as their incredible stilts will carry ...m.

...A myriad of creatures crawl out from under every ...ck and leaf; the garden has turned into a real ...gle. Now the carabus beetle chases his favorite ...ollusks, especially the baby snails which, though ...ey have only recently been hatched in the rain, ...e already racing off to plunder every lettuce ...tch. The guardians of the garden are on the ...tch, too: shrews, mice, birds, moles and hedge-...gs. A million insects hurry hither and thither in ...e unending battle for life. It should never be for-...tten that there are more species of insects than of ...y other living thing, including vegetables!

...No matter how small the garden, it seems a world ...itself to its varied citizens. How tall the plum tree

Golden plover

out such help our gardens and orchards would soon be devastated. Of course, nowadays modern insecticides can get rid of many pests, but in the process they create but another tragedy, for tits, robins and other birds are either poisoned by the insecticides themselves or flee the barren countryside where there is nothing left for them to eat.

...Honey buzzard

Carabus beetle

Crested grebe

AUGUST

When the Curlews Pass Overhead

Emerging from behind a clump of reeds, the great black bull shook off the mud and silt of one of the region's innumerable ponds. Raising his dark bulk against the glowing sky, he disappeared once more into the reeds.

A herd of wild horses lazing under the thin shade of a tamarisk tree barely noticed him; the powerful bull interested them as little as the flocks of birds splashing fitfully in the shallow water.

Here, in the Camargue area of the Rhone river delta in southern France, it was hot as a furnace, and the horizon shimmered in the scorching air.

Scarcely whiter than the sky above, the snowy egrets watched a few wispy clouds drift up from the Mediterranean and along the drainage canals; and pink flamingos, proudly standing aloof on stiltlike legs, kept well away from the groups of plovers on the banks. They all seemed to be waiting, but for what?

Squadrons of gulls passed overhead, shrieking the latest news of the delta to the four corners of the sky. Two crested grebes hove into view from behind a tiny floating island to swim as swiftly away, each grebe with a couple of chicks perched on its back. Father grebe abruptly lowered himself in the water like a submarine, only his head emerging as if it were a periscope. Then, as the chicks scrambled to get aboard their mother, he dove. What a skilled fisherman he is! No larger than a gull, with a long sinuous neck topped by a red and black plumed collar, he spends his entire life on the lagoon . . . in it.

Wading and almost swimming at times, the mammoth bull continued on his way to rejoin his herd under the bushes.

Suddenly a breeze arose to dapple the water surface. The flamingos wandered off to deeper water, their long legs retracting beneath them so that they seemed to float. Actually, they were wading slowly forward, dipping their heads into the shallow water and scraping the bottom with their curious

ooked beaks, so perfectly designed to strain out ud and retain only small worms and tiny shellfish. Night was falling fast when the first curlews apeared overhead, and their strange call could be eard for a long distance. It was time for them to me, for although it was still summer in the Caargue, winter had already begun in Scandinavia here they had laid their eggs.

Suddenly the sky was filled with scythe-shaped ings. The swallows found this a marvelous stopng off place in their voyage, since swarms of mosuitoes buzzed incessantly over the plains.

Almost as though they awaited a signal, the herd wild horses rose as one and galloped off toward e white sand beaches.

At the same time, the flamingos too raised their eads to look about cautiously. In orderly Indian file, ey started to walk, then ran before rising on their ings to fly to a neighboring pond for the night. In e warm August evening, it almost seemed as if me giant hand had strewn rose petals across the ummer sky.

Flamingos

Egret

AUGUST

The Stag Beetle and His Mate

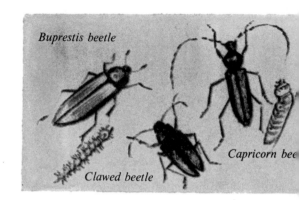

Buprestis beetle

Clawed beetle

Capricorn beetle

Once upon a time two lonely trees stood beside an old stump on the top of a hill. One was an oak, so old it is said that it must have seen five hundred summers. The other was a half-dead pine that stretched its scrawny limbs akimbo in every direction. Long ago the stump must have been a handsome fir, but now it was only a twisted, shapeless mass.

All three were inhabited, however, and every morning a hoopoe flew in garlandlike swoops to pay them each a visit.

The stag beetle and his mate

Stag beetle larva

The old oak was the kingdom of the stag beetle and his mate, who only left their lair at nightfall. Then there'd be a sudden buzzing in the nest before the two ink-dark creatures flew out. From time to time, the rather clumsy male would forget to stay upright, and his enormous mandibles, or jaws, would make him lose his balance. Then the poor creature would fall to the ground with a thud, waving his three pairs of legs in a terrible struggle to get right side up again. Commonly called a stag beetle (due to the shape of his huge mandibles), he is known scientifically as *Lucanus*. Not so well armed as her mate, the female can still give a nasty bite and should only be approached with caution.

She lays her eggs in the rotten wood of trees, and the larvae born of these spend the next four years digging tunnels which, fortunately, don't cause much damage.

Capricorn beetles also attack oak trees, but more destructively, as they prefer the living wood. Their soft, blind larvae chew away, reducing the wood to sawdust. Year after year, as one generation succeeds another, they can eat their way to the very heart of the oak and kill it.

The pine tree had its own group of parasites, Buprestis beetles and bark beetles, who were equally harmful, eating away at the trunk as they did. The clawed beetle preferred the dead wood of the rotten stump.

And so when the hoopoe came flying in she was a welcome sight to the trees, for with her long, curved beak she would peck away in search of tasty larvae. The hoopoe, found in Europe and Africa, feeds on insects on the ground and in trees much as woodpeckers do. This morning, however, she met a we

who couldn't have cared less whether his break-
t wore fur or feathers. Hovering over the oak, the
opoe raised her fine crest and tried to frighten him
ay with cries of "pour-pou-pou." A passing jay
ned in the hubub as the fox's jaws snapped at
pty air. Disappointed and slightly intimidated as
ll, the fox finally slunk off into the grass and van-
ed from sight. By now the sun had awakened the
ckets, and the hoopoe decided to return to the
ods where her favorite breakfast of black ants
aited her.

And deep within the tree, the larvae patiently
ntinued their incessant gnawing and boring into
wood. In time, of course, they would finish their
rk, and then the top of the hill would be bare
cept for the tall grass swaying in the wind.

Hoopoe

e inhabitants of the tree trunks attract the hoopoe, who
urn is watched by the wily fox.

AUGUST

The Ocellate Lizard

The hot sun beats down on the countryside, the wasps peck away happily at the ripe fruit and the brambles drag their clusters of berries on the yellowing grass.

Suddenly, zip! A giant shadow slips between the rocks so fast that he cannot be seen. A dragon might make a shadow like that!

Actually, it's only the ocellate lizard, measuring a strapping two feet six inches from nose to tail. And quite a lizard he is, at that! Like most reptiles he adores the sun; perhaps that's why he favors old ruins and rocky ground in the south of France. He is cold-blooded and his temperature varies according to his surroundings. He loves heat and light and would actually be perfectly content here in his hide-

away were it not for the presence of a grass snak his sworn enemy and rival for the local game.

Invariably our lizard attacks when he happens encounter such a snake, despite the fact that the la ter measures six feet and has a nasty bite. The gra snake can certainly give as much punishment as takes! One might think, though, with all the cricke and other delicious morsels around, that the would be enough for two and that they could li and let live.

For the moment, the lizard is hunting in his ow fashion. When he spies his prey (a fledgling, pe haps, for he is not beyond seizing them from the nests), he stays absolutely motionless, giving us chance to admire his green coat with its ring

Grass snake

Ocellate lizard

pots, or "ocelles," which give him his name. Then, uick as lightning, he springs and grabs the unfortu-ate prey in his jaws, shaking it violently from side o side, beating it on the ground and then swallow-ig it whole.

After this procedure he works his thin tongue round the edge of his mouth like a cat licking its whiskers. Like all other lizards, his tongue is forked nd his body covered with scales.

While this drama took place, the grass snake was ff fishing in the shadow of an old bridge, for she elishes the little frogs who nestle beneath the leaves nd the minnows shimmering in the still pools. nd, when she has the chance, she will also gobble own the little wall lizards. Naturally, they try to scape in a flash, and sometimes succeed in doing o—leaving their tails behind.

Drowsy after her meal, our grass snake slowly slithers her way back toward the ruins on the hill, her track barely visible under the waving tops of wild carrots.

Surprise! The lizard is there, hopefulling waiting between the boulders to spring at her with a snap. But the snake can defend herself, and after a brief scuffle the two adversaries part.

Sometime a bird of prey dives out of the blue and settles the dispute once and for all by summa-rily picking up one of them and flying off.

After all, every hunter is also the hunted. How-ever speedy a lizard of any color or size, it cannot always elude the marten or the wild ferret, and even foxes sometimes succeed in catching lizards when the drought is intense and they come to hunt crick-ets in the dry grass.

AUGUST

The Little Fawn in the August Woods

By the time August comes, few birds are heard singing in the woods.

Late one hot afternoon, a mother roebuck and her fawn wander down to drink from the bubbling brook that runs beneath the hazelnut tree. How handsome they are in their tawny coats, how their dark eyes shine!

The fawn's coat is darker than his mother's, and spotted, almost as if the sun shining through the forest leaves had dappled it with spots of light.

When he was born last May, almost everything that passed by frightened him: the june bugs with their whirring flight into the branches at nightfall, the whiskers of the hare come to see what was happening, even the piercing shriek of the jay in the limbs of the oak tree above.

Does are exceptionally kind mothers, though from time to time they give their fawns well-earned kicks with their forepaws. The young know a great deal by instinct, but in addition they must learn all the lore of the forest, and this is no simple matter.

This evening, for instance, mother and fawn must make sure that the path to the meadow is clear, and the mother seems somewhat anxious. With her keen eyesight and hearing and her excellent sense of smell, she can spot a man far off. Except for the buzzing of the insects, though, the woods seem silent right now.

Still, she is a little worried, and calls, or "bells," to her husband for help. This scoundrel never replies, however. Terrible tempered and ready to "stab" a rival at every opportunity, he treats his family with callous indifference. Providing he gets his daily ten pounds of green forage and tender shoots and can go and come as he pleases in his domain, he's happy.

Now the smell of acrid smoke filters through the air. Perhaps the forest is on fire! Danger! The doe and fawn shake their delicate heads together as if to drive away the unwelcome smell and then trot off under the pines to the tree which their lord and master has marked with his horns as if to say "This far and no farther."

Though he failed to answer the doe's call, the stag is there to welcome them. Perhaps the threat of danger will reunite them. Though they don't yet know what the danger is!

Growth stages of a roebuck's horns

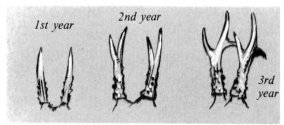

1st year   2nd year   3rd year

A few campers who have pitched their tent on the edge of the woods have unwittingly blocked the deers' passage to their drinking hole. They have lit a campfire, and the breeze has carried the smell of this smoke throughout the woods.

The deer quickly skip off. They stay as far as possible from men, and with good reason. Soon the hunting season will be open, heralding a dark period in their lives.

If providence is kind, however, our little fawn will continue to grow. From a fawn he will graduate to the status of a yearling. Then later he will become a full-fledged stag like his father and proudly bear his six-pronged antlers.

Then he will spring lightly through the woods at dawn, sometimes to stop suddenly, pricking his fine ears up to catch the slightest sound, and swiftly kick an anthill before disappearing gracefully between the trees.

Mosquito

Side view of mosquito

Mosquito larva

Harvest mice

Blackbird

What the Mosquitoes Say

When the ripe fruit hangs heavy on a warm September day, the orchards are apt to be full of insects and rodents of every kind. Gone from the fields is the tiny harvest mouse who can balance on one single wheat stalk as he nibbles away. For him the summer paradise of tall grasses is now ended; his nest fell when the first scythe blade came mowing through the crop. Now he must seek lodging underground, such as in this bed of asters surrounded by buzzing bees, or perhaps beneath that special autumn glory, the dahlias.

Amid the flies, wasps and hornets busily buzzing about the fruit-laden trees is still another kind of insect: the mosquito, born by the millions in the tiniest driblet of water. They too are hard at work, but in another way. They are bothering the gardener, alighting on his neck, his forehead, his bare arms and his hands.

"Awful pests," he mutters as he tries to slap them away, but all his waving and ranting doesn't prevent his getting stung.

The most fascinating feature about this tiny insect, so fragile and so easily crushed, is not its uncanny ability to pierce your tough skin with its trunk and to suck your blood, but the fact that it can talk! Recordings have been made of the different sounds made by mosquitoes in buzzing. One particular noise seems to be a cry of alarm, and if the recording of this sound is played back to mosquitoes, they will frantically buzz off in all directions.

Dolphin

Indeed, it's a well-known fact that animals can exchange all sorts of information. For instance, the blackbird has several calls, each one with a distinct meaning, so that a trained ear can tell from these, even without opening the window, what the weather will be like that day. Another good communicator is the dolphin, whose language is being thoroughly studied now.

Scientists are also trying to find out what bees are saying as they buzz about their hives.

Some animals communicate by other means. They emit chemical substances which serve to signal danger, or simply to convey ordinary information of one sort or another. Deer, for instance, deposit such substances on the bushes bordering their private territories, thus warning intruders to stay away as clearly as if they had posted a "No trespassing" sign.

If a tadpole's skin is touched by the merest thread, he automatically emits a substance into the water that alerts all the other tadpoles in the neighborhood so that they can flee immediately.

And even fish in the sea which swim together in great schools must have some means of signaling one another. We are just beginning to explore this fascinating subject, but we do know that there is no need to vocalize or to make gestures in order to communicate.

But such complicated subjects hardly come to mind as we sit in the autumn garden and lazily watch ripe fruit drop to the ground—to the delight of every bird, insect and rodent in the neighborhood.

Roebuck

Tadpoles

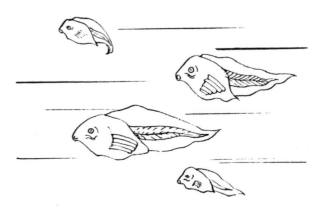

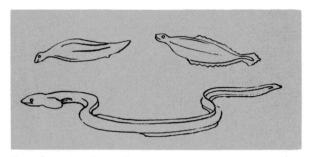

Growth stages of an eel

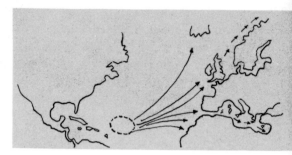

The European eels' migration

SEPTEMBER

The Eel's Long Voyage

When the eel was born under the algae in the warm waters of the mysterious Saragasso Sea, he looked rather like a tiny transparent willow leaf. Yet some strange instinct impelled the tiny eel, along with millions of his kind, to begin a long and hazardous voyage which was to carry him thousands of miles from his birthplace in this mid-Atlantic area toward the coasts of Europe.

Although thousands would perish along the way, so many were born at the same time that thousands of others were bound to survive. Our particular eel's mother laid twenty million eggs alone, and those that managed to endure the rigors of the trip would in time fill the rivers, streams and lakes of Europe. By the time they finally reached the estuaries of the great rivers and began to swim upstream, they would be elvers—about the size and shape of littl[e] minnows.

Having escaped the cruel beaks of herons, as we[ll] as the greedy mouths of trout, chubs, and othe[r] fish, our eel will finally reach the safe, deep water[s] of a pond bordered by reed and frog grass. Here h[e] will prosper and grow.

In four years' time, he'll attain an impressiv[e] length of five feet, his dark green coat will acquire [a] few spangles of orange and silver and his eyes wi[ll] be enormous. He'll also stop eating so much— perhaps simply of his own accord, perhaps due t[o] men hunting off the stream that feeds the lake.

Trout

Chub

Then one dark night when clouds drown the earth ↓low, another mysterious instinct will force the eel ↓t of the pond and into a new series of adventures. ↓aving the water he knows so well, our eel will ↓art off across the fields toward a running stream. ↓ithering snakelike through the grass and mud, ↓'ll be easy prey for owls. But whatever the dan-↓r, he'll keep going until he reaches flowing water. ↓Exhausted from the unaccustomed exertion, the ↓l will let the current carry him downstream. From ↓e stream he'll be carried into the river, and from ↓e river into the sea. Tangled together, hundreds of ↓ls will be swept by the onrushing waters through-↓t the day and night, separating only to hide in the ↓ossy bottoms or along the banks. Many, of course, ↓ll be caught in the nets set for them, to end their ↓ys as delicacies—boiled in an herb-filled stew or ↓rved as smoked eel on toast.

Our eel, however, will reach the estuaries, there ↓ join other males of the species who hadn't swum ↓stream, and together they'll set out for the depths ↓ the Saragasso Sea to perpetuate their species.

Another mystery: no one knows what happens to ↓ female eel once she has laid her eggs. Scientists

have tried to find the answer to this for years, but it still remains an unsolved puzzle. There is only one thing we do know: the mother eel will never be seen again. What secrets nature keeps for itself!

AUTUMN

Avocet

Heron

Mallard

SEPTEMBER

The Water Birds' Useful Beaks

During the autumn equinox, wild waves dash their foamy crests over the coasts of Europe. In the gray, cloud-flecked sky above, migrating birds fly over by the thousand on their way to warmer climes. During this same time, hundreds and thousands of water birds gather in shallow swamps along the Atlantic shoreline of France. It is an unforgettable sight, and as this coastal region is a wildlife preserve, nothing disturbs the wild cries of the gulls or the wind's whistling across the vast plains. Now is a good opportunity to take a close look at the fascinating collection of strange-named birds who gather in such numbers along these estuaries, lagoons and beaches. Let's examine especially the odd-shaped beaks from which many of them derive their names.

First of all comes a joyous group of oystercatchers in their black and white liveries; their orange beaks stand out in vivid contrast to the drab surroundings. These beaks have acquired an impressive reputation, but even though it's certain that they are useful in digging for an errant shellfish or two among the mussels living on the rocks and in the sand, they wouldn't be very effective in actually opening an oyster—even assuming that the bivalve were willing to cooperate!

Present also is the slim and elegant avocet whose upward-turning beak serves mainly to peck about in mud or shallow water in search of tiny mollusks.

By contrast, the wild and elusive curlew has a beak which curves downward and enables it to ferret out dainty morsels stubbornly burrowed in the earth.

The fish-preying birds—gray or blue herons more often found along the Mediterranean than in these northern waters—have heavy swordlike beaks with sharp, teethlike prongs that enable them to keep a firm grasp on the fish they has speared.

Spoonbills, ducks and other birds among the Anatidae family feature fringed, flat bills which act as sieves, allowing the water to drain away as they keep a grip on their prey.

Nature is indeed marvelous, bestowing to the scavengers of the seashore—the sandpipers, redshanks, and snipe darting about the waters' edge—beaks which are ideally suited to acquire each bird's particular form of food or to perform some special type of work. And, of course, some beaks serve as weapons. Rare is the bird that can stand up to a heron's dagger!

As for the short, blunt beaks of our garden songbirds, we can truthfully say that these, in addition to being perfectly suited to their way of life, serve also as musical instruments that could be the envy of any water bird, none of whom can boast of a particularly attractive song.

For though the gulls can whistle like a finch and even hoot like an owl, who could ever hear them amidst the loud roar of the Atlantic breakers?

Gulls call to one another incessantly, to let it be known that a trawler is pulling into port or that, due to a storm at sea, their fellows would be better off in the swamp; they are indeed courageous birds. The people of Sweden consider them good luck and smile at the sight of these great white birds come to peck in the furrows of their fields like common sparrows.

Black-headed gull

Curlew

Sanderlings

Oystercatcher

SEPTEMBER

The Owl and His Larder

September is the harvest month, when fruit ripens to be picked or to fall from the trees, and it is the season when both men and animals lay in supplies for the winter. As in spring, the grass turns green again under the fall rains, long-stemmed daisies and mint shoot up, mushrooms sprout under forest shade and new moss covers the rotting tree stumps.

Jay

Squirrel

At this time, when everyone is looking ahead to the coming bad weather, there's a concerted effort to see that nothing is wasted. Just as men gather and press grapes to make wine to fill their kegs, just as housewives on the farm save apples and pears to make pots of jam, so animals gather and stow away their grains, roots and berries.

In the forests as in the fields, where the Christmas geese fatten on crickets, there is a furtive hurrying and scurrying everywhere. Squirrels with nuts in their cheeks leap in great bounds to their secret storage places, the jays bury acorns in the ground and rows of ants carry innumerable seeds. (It is said that the clever ants know how to prevent the seeds from sprouting in their underground granaries.)

Though the hedgehog doesn't actually stock apples on his spines as one tall story has it, he does stuff himself with food in order to build up a solid layer of fat before hibernating under the leaves.

And the very busiest of all are little rodents. In Germany, hamsters store vast quantities of roots in their complicated burrows, and in Sweden the furry-coated lemmings also lay in a supply. (But

Hedgehog

when there are too many lemmings for the food supply, hordes of them emigrate to the nearby sea and drown themselves there.) Throughout Europe the voles gather seeds.

What a boon all this activity is for the short-eared owl with his yellow, black-rimmed eyes. His entire life depends on the voles, and his every action hinges on their prosperity. When the neighborhood abounds in voles, the hen owl makes her nest large enough to accommodate a dozen eggs. If few voles

Hamster

Hamster's burrow

Owl

owl is famous for his deadly aim. And since voles are so lightweight, the owl must have at least one every day. Not that this poses any problem, for the short-eared owl hunts night and day. And even if voles should become extinct, he can always satisfy his hunger with shrews—or even, in a pinch, with large insects.

Like the wolf and the North American and Scandinavian wolverine, or glutton, which follows herds of reindeer, the owl follows these rodents so as to have a perpetual supply on hand. Theirs is a living larder unlike many others.

are about, she will lay no more than four eggs. If, for one reason or another, voles completely disappear, the short-eared owls disperse in every direction to wander thousands of miles if need be, slowly searching the swamps and plains until they find another area blessed in voles. As the owls swoop swiftly over the bushes, their round faces strike terror in the hearts of all the rodents; the short-eared

Wolverine

Ants

The Bear in the Mountains

The brown bear of the Pyrenees blinks his ti 
piglike eyes to discourage the annoying flies buzzi 
around them, yawns broadly and, placing his pa 
comfortably on his fat belly, settles down for  
nap against an old mossy stump. Life is inde 
pleasant at siesta time.

The fact that only about sixty of his species a 
left in the world does not seem to trouble him or 
prevent his enjoyment of the September rains in  
native mountains, the chain running between Spa 
and France. Early this morning he breakfasted on 
bellyfull of mushrooms (plus the juicy fat slu 
taking shelter under them) and he followed this fi 
course with as many wild berries as he could fi 
under the towering pines. This bear dotes on frui 
and berries; they help restore the sheen to his thi 
fur (which can become a bit bedraggled during t 
warm summer weather). Autumn is his favorite se 
son, and though he may seem blindly greedy in t 
vast quantities he devours, he's really quite sele 
tive as to quality. He knows his mountains as w 
as he knows the palms of his huge forepaws;  
knows just when the frogs hop through the mea 
ows, and when it's the best time to fish for trout 
the mountain lakes where the tawny local catt 
come for water. His keen sense of smell unerring 
sends him straight to every gastronomic delight 
the region. In the woods he loves to paw wild hon 
from the bees' nests and will even lumber down 
attack the hives of nearby farms, but he spen 
most of his time in the deep woods where even  
imposing 450-pound bulk seems puny against t 
colossal mountain background.

He pays little attention to the other animals, e 
cept perhaps for his mate, to whom he pays cou 
for a brief period in October before totally ignori 
her for the rest of the year. Loudly crashing throug 
the undergrowth, he frightens off the game bir 

hich are more patiently stalked by foxes and other rnivores.

Meandering here and there, he will nibble away at lything tasty that crosses his path—a snail here, a rge insect there. He'll plow through anthills, dig in e earth and carefully turn over stones to see hat's crawling under them. Then, tired of this rty work, he'll groom himself by nicely cleaning s fur or sharpening his long claws against the nk of a tree.

When the first wild walnuts, acorn and hazel nuts ll to the ground in September, he can never get ough. In fact, he needs to build up a solid layer fat, for winters are long and rigorous in the Pyre-es Mountains. While his sleep is not deep, he re-xes thoroughly in his den, curled up into a ball d doing nothing more strenuous than licking his ws from time to time. He could, of course, gather in a store of nuts, but bears don't seem to go in for this sort of project.

Though he stays quietly in his den today, the faintest noise will arouse his curiosity and mistrust. And with good reason! After all, there was a time when he fought with men for the possession of these same caves, and only recently many an inno-cent nut- and berry-eating bear has paid the penalty for resembling his lamb-killing brother, the cave bear. He has a good memory, and can still recall the sound of gunfire echoing through the forest.

Fortunately for him, though, the Pic d'Ossau area where he lives is now a protected game reserve, so perhaps he will become less suspicious eventually.

After his nap the bear gets up, breaks off a nearby branch, carefully peels it and sucks out the sweet sap. Then, the first course over, he ambles off to his favorite spot for a main dish of mushrooms.

SEPTEMBER

The Badger

As the sun rose on this September morn, a pink nose peeked inquisitively from under a bush. It was followed by a white face marked by two large black bands running all the way from tufted ears to shiny black eyes. And after this curious head came a squat, dark-gray body—it was a badger. Now he began to trot along, nodding his head from side to side as if well satisfied with last night's hunt for muscat grapes.

The badger is a grumpy and solitary individualist who seems to detest everyone, even avoiding his own mate most of the time and leaving to her the entire job of rearing their young.

For a month now, this particular badger had been making the most of harvest time with its ripening fruit and honey-filled hives. The poor bees must have thought him a queer kind of bear from the brusque way he invaded their home—without, apparently, minding their stings at all.

Leaving the tiresome chore of nut-gathering to squirrels and voles, the badger had built up his larder more directly—in the form of a thick layer of fat on his body. Now he felt quite prepared to pass the winter in his comfortable, warm lair lined with dry hay.

Since the time hadn't quite come for him to hibernate, he would wander back to the vineyard for a delicious cluster of golden grapes. Like wasps, thrushes and foxes, the badger has a weakness for these delicacies and would continue to enjoy them until harvest time.

Oddly enough, that very morning his greed had saved his life. Tired of the harm done his crops by the destructive badger (whose powerful claws indiscriminately uprooted vegetables in the search for grubs and roots, and who also pillaged his fields and hives), the farmer had determined to smoke him out of his den.

But the badger was a crafty animal, with a sense of smell far sharper than either his hearing or his eyesight. One sniff of the air immediately told him what was afoot, and accordingly he made tracks in the opposite direction. To the farmer's disappointment, all that came out of the badger's hole was smoke and then more smoke.

Anyway, it was time for the badger to go to see his wife and children, who lived in a lair on the other side of the hill. As we have said, he was an infrequent visitor there, but autumn being the mating season for badgers, it seemed the thing to do.

Outside their home, the mother badger and her pups were warming themselves. Mediocre head of the family though he was, at least he had helped to build this home, digging the tunnels with his powerful claws and thoughtfully providing plenty of emergency exits, all facing south. He had even defended it against a marauding fox who had tried to appropriate the well-planned abode. The fox had learned, to his chagrin, that a badger's skin is loose enough for him to turn from almost any position and bite back.

There in the sunlight the badger family basked contentedly. Sometimes they napped, sometimes they conversed in grunts, as their fancy dictated. At this time of year they really lacked nothing. There was plenty of food about to gorge on and thus thicken the roll of fat which would enable them to sleep steadily all through the long winter (unlike the marmot, who wakes to make an occasional appearance in balmy weather).

But when they finally did wake up, thin and emaciated and wracked with hunger, the sap would be rising, the buds about to burst open.

All nature would then be reawakening and the badgers, once again, would be more than ready to make the most of it.

117

*A solitary turtle dove waits to join
the wood pigeons on their way south.*

The Pigeons
of October

Rain fell torrentially in the valley between the hillsides.

From his nest in an oak tree, the turtle dove sprang into the air, spreading his wings above his head for a second before soaring off. He loved nice warm rains, but nowadays they were no longer quite so warm. Flying in a great circle, he returned to his oak tree to scan the cloudy horizon. Yes, October was definitely here.

That meant he must make a decision. Would he migrate southward or, like last year, spend the winter here in the woods? Actually, he had little trouble making up his mind. Last year a poacher had shot down his mate, and without her the snow felt even colder. He would go south.

Above the hills, the air began to sing with the beating of a thousand wings. Wood pigeons were on

the move, heading south through the rain, their dark gray coats glistened like wet slate.

The turtle dove decided that he would join their group and travel with them.

But the flock did not alight immediately; first a scout carefully inspected the terrain, investigating the slightest shadow for anything suspicious. All seemed in order.

Reassured by the scout's report, the other pigeons thankfully settled down under the oaks. They were famished. With their heads raised to reveal white patches on either side of their necks, they did not even break up the acorns with their beaks but, with rapid movements of their pale pink gullets, they swallowed them whole.

As the rain stopped, a ray of sun shone through the leaves, illuminating the oak trees and creating

the illusion that the trees were abloom with for-get-me-nots and violets.

The turtle dove watched the pigeons alight and feed on the upper branches, then quiet down for the night. He too closed his shining eyes, tucked his orange beak under his wing and slept.

dove who nested in their midst. After all, these woods were his home, and so they were, in a way, his guests. As rain commenced again, the autumn-red leaves began to drift wetly to the ground. And so life went on, until one evening a blast of gunfire echoed through the wood; the entire flock took off

During the warm and balmy days that followed, the migrating wood pigeons made the most of their stop-over, hungrily gorging themselves on tasty beech-nuts, acorns and juniper berries (which left them a bit tipsy).

Then, resting their beaks on plump breasts, they cooed tenderly, utterly ignoring the strange turtle

and, with a tremendous flutter of wings, headed south.

Cruel nets had been stretched in the pine barrens of the Basque country in the western Pyrenees, but the pigeons flew high and managed to elude them. Leaving his rustic nest to the martens and squirrels, the turtle dove happily followed in their wake.

Crayfish

OCTOBER

Kingfisher and Crayfish

A kingfisher sat on the branch of a dead tree, perch that he far preferred to the slim shoots droop ing over the water which prevented him from ge ting a flying start on his plunge into the river for th small freshwater fish.

The pale October sun glinted off his proud re breast and his colorful blue coat with its spray tiny white dots. No matter how beautiful, thoug the mere sight of his squat body and daggerlike bea spread panic among the small fry in the stream.

What the kingfisher especially craved at the moment was crayfish, for he knew that, like all other hard-shelled creatures, at this time of year they had to shed their armor and so would be defenseless. However, the nearest crayfish, who inhabited a dark tunnel under a mossy rock, was wise in her ways and expected to live a full sixty years, as had her grandmother. She had observed the kingfisher's swift shadow on the surface of the water above and cautiously decided to stay in her hiding place until nightfall. Actually, her enemy didn't know where she lived; he also lived in a hole under an alder. He had only noticed that, all summer long, fishermen kept dredging up crayfish in their trapping nests. And now, with his tiny claws gripping the dead branch, he watched and waited for the crayfish to emerge. She too was waiting as long as she could, but her old shell was stifling. Rubbing her legs together, tumbling on her back and curling her tail, she writhed spasmodically and then rested. Now a sudden gust of wind brought a shower of dead leaves down onto the still water.

With a last mammoth effort, the crayfish forced off her shell, carefully pulling her head out the end and withdrawing her feet one by one. She took a big jump backward and finally shed her confining armor. What a relief!

But now she was soft and vulnerable, at the mercy of every enemy, including the eels. Of course, she was used to this, having shed her shell eight times the first year, five times the second and since then, in adulthood, only once a year. Did she sense that a storm was coming on and that the brown leaves swirling downstream would protect her from the kingfisher's searching eyes? In any case, she prudently remained motionless in her tunnel.

Thinking he saw a crayfish bobbing along in the water, the kingfisher dove straight away. But alas for him, when he came up again it was only an unappetizing old shell that he held in his beak. With a piercing cry of disappointment, he dropped the shell in disgust and returned to his nest under the river bank.

He would be back, of course, for he always fished along the same section of the stream, but by that time the crayfish's armor would have had a chance to harden and she'd be able to swim away quickly, propelled by her strong tail. Anyway, by then she might have changed her hole.

And, if her luck held, she would live twenty times longer than the kingfisher.

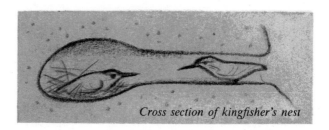

Cross section of kingfisher's nest

OCTOBER

The Barn Owl in the Church Tower

Night falls softly over the village rooftops and th
rising moon bathes the surrounding countryside in
cold light. The whole world seems asleep, but is
really? Aloft on silent wings, a strange bird hove
over the shadowy gardens, then edges imperceptib
toward the fields. Those two unblinking eyes set
a frightening white mask belong to the barn ow
most bizarre and beautiful of all the nocturnal bir
of prey, with its finely speckled white breast a
coat of golden buff. It can fly silently as a ghost
its rounded wings and hover lengthily in mid-air.

Clover is still in bloom on this October evenin
making the air fragrant after yesterday's rain. Th
tantalizing scent has attracted a young rabbit wh
loves the little white blooms and the leaves th
close up at night. He hops along, sniffing excited!
Not far away, a field mouse with similar tast
gnaws away at the clover roots he has uncovered.

And high above, their enemy the barn owl circl
menacingly.

Under an oak tree, a little rabbit comes across
delicious red-capped mushroom, and he nibbles awa
sitting on his haunches and rubbing his no
pleasurably.

Just then the field mouse thinks he hears a susp
cious noise; an acorn has fallen and rolled over t
leaves, and he goes to investigate.

Zooming down with incredible speed, the ba
owl seizes the little rodent in its talons and flies
with it to a nearby treetop.

Seeing the ominous shadow passing overhead, the little rabbit scampers for cover, frightened half to death.

Let us not waste our sympathy on the little field mouse, though, for all the diurnal and noctural birds of prey in the world would not be enough to prevent field mice, dormice, voles and shrews from destroying our crops. The balance of nature must be maintained.

For one reason or another, perhaps because the rains have flooded their nests, there aren't many rodents about this year, and being aware of this, the barn owls laid only two eggs in their nest in the church tower. By now the young owlets have flown from the nest and are hunting hundreds of miles away. This evening, like every evening, the mother owl feels ravenous and must hunt for hours to even half satisfy her appetite.

Barn owls are fairly well known these days, but not too long ago peasants walking to the fields at dawn would hear the owls' piercing shrieks overhead, glance up at the odd shapes and, believing them to be some kind of ghosts, take to their heels.

The raw October wind increases its tempo to spin the weather vane on the steeple. Inside the tower, two fierce sentinels stand motionless on a beam as they hear the morning services. Then, with their eyes only half closed, the barn owls doze—perhaps dreaming of tomorrow's hunting and an endless procession of mice.

OCTOBER

The Glory of the Autumn Woods

The splendor of autumn leaves is matched by a cock pheasant's glorious plumage.

This particular pheasant had been hatched by a common barnyard hen, then brought up by a farmer who provided the very best ant eggs and appetizing mashes to make him grow. But of course he could remember none of this, for he'd been let loose in the hunting reserve almost four years ago.

A bountiful nature seems to have lavished ever gift upon him as far as appearances go, and he ful exploits his beauty. With his green head highlighte by red cockades, bronze and black-speckled feathe and long elegant tail, he has no trouble acquiring harem of lady pheasants. None of them aspire match his gaudy plumage, and their dull live blends perfectly with the dead leaves and earth tha they squat on to lay their eggs. The future of th race depends on these drab creatures, for our gauc father pheasant hasn't the slightest interest in h

Nature has endowed cock pheasants with highly colorful plumage; yet the hen's drab feathers make concealment easier.

ood and pays no attention to them at all; indeed,
: is altogether a quarrelsome, opinionated beast.
's just as well that the hens appear to be almost
visible as they sit over their clutches of fourteen
ive-green eggs. There are so many deadly enemies
the woods—and now it is the autumn hunting sea-
n when all the beasts and birds of the field, above
l pheasants, must be especially wary.

How simple and gay life was just a week ago.
he cock pheasant could display his fine plumage,
rut proudly along his private walks, peck at succu-
nt seeds in the fields, cut sweet shoots with his
ort sharp beak, scratch the earth with his strong
aws and perch overnight in an oak tree quite
fely.

But, alas, this morning, despite the heavy rain,
blast of gunfire rips the silence of the woods and
ives terrified partridges to shelter in the grass.

And every partridge hunter would also shoot pheasant, of course.

Experience has taught its lessons well; our pheasant must keep his wits about him when dogs are involved. A pheasant rising in a frantic flapping of wings is often a lost bird. Though he can run swiftly on the ground, he is heavy and flies badly.

Slipping under the ferns, which leave pearls of dew on his glistening coat, he makes for the bramble patch with its barely turning leaves, and then heads toward the little swamp where his trail will be lost. No sooner has he tucked his tail under an overhanging bramble than he comes face to face with another of the hunted, a hare hidden between two clumps of earth and as obviously frightened as he is himself.

And who knows the outcome? Everything depends on luck. But whatever happens, even if one ends up in a humble stew and the other elegantly served under glass, come springtime there will be plenty of striped chicks to drink the dew from fresh grassy spears, and many more pretty rabbits with soft, velvety ears.

The gamekeepers will see to it that there's enough game left next year both to delight bird lovers and to satisfy the crueler instincts of huntsmen.

OCTOBER

Behind the Shutters

The long-eared mother bat had lived in fear behind the shutters of a window in her new home in the village since her offspring had been eaten by the polecat (a kind of wild ferret).

Who could have imagined that the frog-eating polecat would have wandered into her deep cave in the mountains just at that fatal instant when the baby bat let go of its mother, fell away in free flight and broke its fall with tiny outstretched wings?

Poor little bat was only a mouthful for the masked intruder—who, of course, would eat almost anything, including vipers. Polecats aren't at all discriminating and, like hedgehogs, they have no fear of a viper's fangs.

While the tiny bat was still blind and his ears were soft and pressed close against his body, the mother bat had carried him along with her on her hunting trips.

She felt a little lonely without him, but before long she became accustomed to her solitude and had moved away from the cave and into the village.

Every evening when the apollo and sylvan butterflies closed their wings for the night, she set out on her rounds. Seeing her, the villagers would look up and say "Hello, there's a bat," and they would be right, of course, though scientists would call her a *Plecotus auritus,* or long-eared bat, and with good

Polecat

126

eason. Her ears were enormous and so sensitive a
adar set that she never bumped into anything, but
unted and flew through the darkened streets in
omplete safety. Cursed with a thirst to match her
remendous appetite, she drank the way swallows
o, skimming over the water's surface.

The polecat lived near the village, too, and like
he bat only hunted at night, making sure that the

and ducks waddling down to the ponds. It would be
just too bad if he were trapped.

As for the bat, she and others like her would migrate to a cave in North African Morocco, where
they would spend the winter months huddled together by the thousands, hanging upside down from
the roof of a cave, enveloped in their wings.

And while they were away in warmer climes, the
deserted cave near the village would be occupied by
two species of butterflies, the first to announce that
spring was on its way.

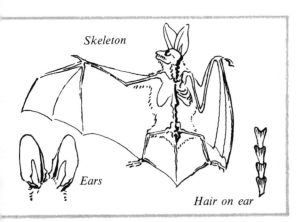

ong-eared bat

wnsfolk didn't get a glimpse of his shaggy coat
nd stumpy legs.

Poking his flat-nosed face out of a rabbit burrow
at he had appropriated for himself, the polecat
autiously peered around before setting off after
is favorite game—frogs, lizards and moths. From
me to time he would visit voles' burrows and occa-
onally he would roll in the grass, showing the dark
ur on his belly which contrasted so curiously with
is otherwise tawny coat. He had a mate, of course,
a hollow willow tree near a stream edged with
ellow-centered caltha lilies, but he was rather a
oor husband and father, ignoring wife and children
ike.

Like the bat, he preferred to hunt alone.

He liked fat pigeons and chickens, too—but not to
e point of losing his head and slaughtering them
holesale as a marten does.

October is a dangerous month to go near farms;
ith plenty of game about, traps are set. But there
ere hens pecking their way out toward the woods

Partridges

NOVEMBER

The Partridge in the Snow

The covey of little partridges assembled under the watchful eye of their white-bosomed mother. They stretched their tiny necks out toward the fields, but then hastily pulled them back. Really, it was too cold this November dawn to do anything but huddle close together for warmth.

Eighteen young chicks in two batches made a sizable family. Mother hen had certainly had her work cut out for her last summer. Were it not for a certain marten, there'd have been twenty chicks—but luckily birds don't know how to count.

Pressing close to one another and protected by their soft feathers, the partridges could cope with the gusty, cold wind that had induced them to seek shelter among the reeds near the lake.

But the frost was something else!

Yesterday they had pecked their way through whole field trying to find a lost seed here, a lit dried grass there, and, by digging determinedly few occasional ant eggs. And they had also seen hare on his morning rounds. The mother partrid watched his movements carefully, for his behavi often revealed hidden perils; she knew that whoev hunts the hare hunts partridge as well.

On this particular morning the mother partrid scratched at the hard, fresh snow in vain; spindly little legs lacked the strength to bre through its crust. And through the tall grass s could see the fox passing by like a red shadc How awful it was to be both cold and afraid!

While the appearance of a fox might mean dea for one partridge, a continued frost meant inevi ble starvation for them all.

But here was the hare again, bounding purpo fully into a furrow before he disappeared. WI had attracted him there? A bit of bark, a twig?

The best thing to do was to remain conceal near the frozen lake as far as possible from the f seeking game in the woods.

Fox

...wing his way through the snow, the hare makes a path ...t the partridges will follow.

Sad to say, the next day their situation was even ...re critical, for the earth had turned hard as ...ne. Yet they had to find *something* to eat. In des-...ration, nineteen tiny bodies clad in ash-gray rus-...-dotted feathers emerged from their hiding place ...d in single file headed toward the bushes. Though ...was daytime, the countryside remained shrouded ... fog.

...Perhaps the ground would be a trifle softer under ... brambles. Perhaps in the bottom of a ditch or ...der some dead leaves there might still be a few ...oons, a pupa or even a bit of grass—at this point ...ey'd be grateful for anything at all.

Suddenly reappearing from some secret hiding place, the hare started to dig under the plum tree. His powerful paws made the snow fly.

Unknowingly, he had saved the partridges' lives. One by one they followed the narrow path he cut before he leapt under a bush, disappearing as suddenly as he had arrived.

Nineteen infinitesimal beaks pecked avidly at the grass he had uncovered. With any luck, the weather would be warmer tomorrow. But no matter what fate had in store, the mother partridge would stay with her chicks until February and share their lot, whether good or bad.

Snowy owl

Goosander

NOVEMBER

The Swans of Lapland

Well before Parisian school children start buying the season's first roasted chestnuts from street vendors, the wild reindeer of Lapland have been obliged to abandon their favorite food, the tender buds of the dwarf willow. Filtering down from their summer home in the mountains, they now nibble at the not-so-tasty grass and lichen that grows on the tundra. Perhaps they had some mysterious advance knowledge that winter would come early this year. Heaven knows, winter always comes early enough in these latitudes where the last winter snow falls in March and the first winter storms of the following season dot the ground with white in September. But the reindeer, of course, are used to this.

To the swans and their young cygnets, however, time doesn't seem to mean a thing. The young birds paddle happily along beside their mother, and as the goosander living in the old pine tree beside the lake can testify, all five of the youngsters born late

that summer are progressing nicely. The goosander had watched them grow from balls of fluffy grey down to their present size, had seen them float like white angels on the still waters of the lake. now the goosander too was gone, following cousins the ducks and geese as they flew V-formation toward warmer lands.

Now the great snowy owl has come down from the mountains in search of lemmings and other rodents. This too is a signal of coming frost, and swans may not ignore it much longer.

Realizing at last that the winter will be severe, mother swan decides that the time has come to st south. She has only waited until the young cygne wings are strong enough, for the journey is long a arduous.

Now they must all spread their great white wing and with a steady beat fly southward down coast. They will stop from time to time, of cour but only when absolutely necessary.

Blinded by the snow, the swans land one eveni to seek shelter where the reindeer are nibbling the forest moss. Huddled together with their lo horns interlaced, the deer are perfectly warm und their shaggy coats, and their sweet-smelling brea rises to form a cloud of mist over their heads. I spite the cold, they are as comfortable as any he of cows in their stable.

...ming

...en the snow starts to fall and the lakes freeze over, it is ... for the wild swans to start south.

Not so lucky are the swans, however, as they crowd together for warmth in the shelter of a tree. The youngsters are half dead from hunger and exhaustion, but they follow their parents' example and dutifully tuck their heads under their wings. Thanks to their thick feathers and underlying down, they too can keep warm, but for this night at least the young cyngnets will have to sleep without first having supper.

Tomorrow they will continue on their way, perhaps as far as the Rhine River in Germany or the Thames in England. Indeed, if the winter is really bad, they may even fly onward to the warmth of the Rhone delta in southern France.

NOVEMBER

The Otters
in the River

Oddly enough, the icy waters of the Rhone seem to be boiling like a cauldron. Brrr, how cold the dawn mists are along the river this morning!

Overhead, a lone curlew passes, singing his mournful song, while a few barren poplars, bent by gusts of winter wind, add to the dreariness.

Then all at once, near the river banks, a flat, cat-like head with bristling whiskers pops up from a whirlpool. It is soon followed by a long, black, shining body which springs onto the bank and then turns. It is an otter, watching to see whether its young have followed.

Yes—there they are! Almost adults now, but as ready for games as ever. With backs arched, they trot along like basset hounds, then disappear unde a fringe of roots laid bare by the autumn flood Now they dive into the shallow water. Silver bubbles float away from their fur as they swim alon; their pink noses break the surface and then the hoist themselves onto the pebble beach. Here the roll around, play hide and seek among the branch and then dive into the water again as noiselessly frogs. Suddenly the winter scene is no long dreary.

True, otters do dine well, though not so well the disgruntled fishermen say who accuse them devouring everything edible in the river. Main they'll have eaten ailing trout: the old femal who, unable to lay eggs any longer, simply lu along the banks decimating the minnow populatio Otters dine almost exclusively on sick fish and frog which they love, and at times even on crayfish a moles.

Long ago these otters had abandoned their tu nel-like lair with its underwater entrance, partly d to their wanderlust and partly because they felt th a new hunting ground was needed.

Now, the eldest otter sneezes, then slips silently into the water. It's time for a nap, so the otter family will retrace their journey back to the little island where the mother otter used to fish after she had hidden her babies under a clump of earth.

But that, of course, was many months ago, in the springtime, when the orioles were singing so melodiously in the trees.

It's virtually impossible to keep track of otters because of their irregular habits. One day they may go after eels, a rather slow fish they have a weakness for, and the next day they may drag a sleeping duck down from its nest of reeds, though this is more unusual. Sometimes they commandeer a badger's former home or sleep in the hollow of a willow tree. Otters are rugged animals, and they are prudent as well as playful. Their very favorite sport, and one they practice daily, is sliding down mud banks. They will indulge in this pastime over and over, a dozen or a hundred times in succession.

When it's time to stop, the mother otter will utter a strange whistling call which the little ones will answer with catlike meowings.

An otter's den

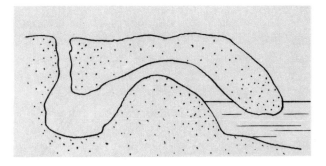

Tree creeper

NOVEMBER

Our Bad-Weather Friends

Now that the autumn leaves have all fallen, most of the springtime songbirds have decided to spurn our gardens and woods. Luckily, others have come down from the mountains and from the north to console us.

Migrating birds headed south are passing overhead and their strange, hoarse cries convey the unmistakable message that winter is on its way. What fun it would be to follow the southbound travelers in their trek toward the lands of perpetual spring where flowers can bloom untouched by frost. Yet what dangers these birds must encounter on their journey! And as the hunting season is open, the fox slinking through the undergrowth snacks on whatever the dogs have left behind or whatever the tide has washed ashore.

How barren the trees are! These former sanctuaries where birds could once hide now hold no secrets. We can see right through the branches, and have to be grateful for whatever birds still linger. On the oak tree, thank goodness, a solitary thrush is inspired by a ray of sunlight to sing out its brave defiance of the coming winter.

The tree creeper, who crawls in a spiral up the trunks, explores each cranny in the bark with his long curved beak. The goldcrest, alert as he is small, raises his crest like an orange banner in the larches. Leaping from branch to branch, he gobbles one last fly. When frost hardens the yellow and brown leaves that dot the forest floor, he will carefully turn over each one with his tiny claws to quickly pluck any insect hidden there with his beak. Sometimes he'll find an unexpected treat, such as the remains of a bumblebee left behind by some scavenging crows.

Oddly enough, the jay, who remained relatively quiet all summer, now dominates the woods with his strident note and is answered in kind by the magpies.

Family groups of crowlike rooks hunt the last of the ground-dwelling wagtails, who seem to beat time with their tails as if to say—"One, two, three, let's be off to the sunny south." As the temperature drops, more and more rooks congregate together. Bearing in mind that it takes half an ounce of grain daily to keep each one of them fed, we can under-

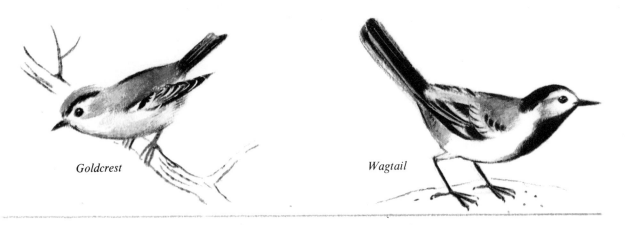

Goldcrest

Wagtail

and that the sheer hundreds of them must mean ns of seed lost. No wonder indignant farmers ring up the rooks they manage to kill, hoping to ighten off the rest. Yet no animal (except for some sects) is completely harmful, and we must remember that the rooks also do away with the destructive hite worm and vermin they uproot in the fields.

How wonderful it is that not all the birds have bandoned us; that we still have blackbirds, thrush-s, starlings and pigeons in the garden, that the oodpeckers still laugh and fly between the hollow trees. Our faithful winter friends are there to give us good cheer throughout the cold weather.

Never mind that the leaves have fallen. Pert little birds still soar into the tingling fall air and gladden our hearts with merry chirping. And though it's no longer nesting time, of course, a strange kind of common bond unites the chaffinches, tits, greenfinches and robins so that they chummily fly off together to look for food, and perch in rows feather to feather, along low-lying branches, as the cruel wind whistles through the woods.

Blue tit

Chaffinch

Robin

135

NOVEMBER

The Island Pony

Pony

Between the rocky coast of Scotland and the deep Norwegian fjords lie the Shetland Islands, little storm-tossed dots on an angry sea where indomitable puffins and skuas and other sea birds nest. And here, one day, a tiny pony was born.

Ponies are not sea birds, of course, but like all the hardy inhabitants of the Shetlands, they too must face the wild winds that toss foam from the waves way up over the sparse grass of these desolate shores.

But nothing fazes these sturdy little beasts—neither the howling November wind nor the white foam nor the icy cold. With their shiny round hooves firmly planted on the peat, they like to deeply inhale the freezing salt wind that blows down from Iceland, as well as from the vast Arctic Ocean beyond.

And though angry gales may whip through their tangled manes and make their long tails wave like flags against their flanks, they remain unaffected, as much a part of the landscape as the local sheep whose fleece nearly touch the ground.

Born in April when the island meadows are abloom with tiny wildflowers, and frisky lambs gambol around their mother, the infant ponies are dry in half an hour and soon walking on their short, strong legs. From ten weeks on they follow their mother everywhere, and for six months they drink her warm milk.

Not many little ponies stay in the Shetlands. Over a century ago Queen Victoria decreed that there should be pony carts at Windsor Castle, and since then the little horses have become popular throughout the world.

Some are sold to riding masters who carefully train them to carry happy children on their backs. Some are bought by farmers who use the ponies to pull carts during the week and then race them on Sundays, for they also make wonderful trotters.

But none of the little ponies has any idea of where his future lies. One of them stamps with his hooves at the frozen earth in search of a salty blade or two of grass. He has no warm blanket like the dark-eyed cows of Jersey, nor does he sport a long, shaggy coat like the local Highland cattle. What he does have, though, may be even better—an under down which makes his coat snug and waterproof. However wet the coming winter, he'll be well prepared. He looks up at some brown gulls floating effortlessly above, then at the seals playing in the surf. Peat smoke billows from the low farmhouse where women busily spin and knit their famous Shetland wool.

The pony shakes his mane, hearing his mother calling him from behind a low stone wall. Ears pricked up, eyes bright with mischief, he gallops off to join her, his head held high as if to say, "Who cares about the cold; snowflakes are just like little white flies I can trample underfoot."

Soon our alert and amusing little pony will be leaving his home, never to return. Fortunately, though, there will always be ponies on these northern storm-tossed isles.

Sheep

Puffin   *Skua*   *Seal*

The First Snow

Only two days ago it was warm; yesterday it was rather chilly, and today it's one of those typically dreary November mornings. It's hard to believe that snow has actually come. But there, filling the horizon as it stretches toward Spain, is a flurry of little white flakes. The first snow had started to fall on the Pyrenees Mountains which separate France and Spain.

Naturally enough, it was a signal for children to dawdle on their way to school, for the horses to shake their manes as they galloped joyfully through the fields and for even the placid cows to speed the tempo of their nibbling along the hedges.

The wild goats have left the blue ice of the glaciers to seek refuge in the forests.

It seemed absolutely ridiculous that snow should
first fall while the leaves were still on the trees and
barely touched with russet. The snow was bound to
melt, of course, for it wasn't winter yet. The sparrows agreed about that as they chattered among the
large wet flakes; and the old oak tree, waving its
leafy green crest as if to shake off the white crystals,
seemed to be informing the greenfinches, coal tits
and robins that the *real* snow was still high up in
the mountains.

Hare

But what were the poor animals doing up there?
The wild goats had prudently left the blue ice of the
glaciers to seek refuge in the forests and now were
making their way down, headed for the pines and
the lower pastures.

Exhilarated by the sight of the large wet flakes,
the yearling kids leapt with joy and tried to lick the
white feathers swirling around them. This delicious
new snow was quite unlike what they had encountered during the summer, the tired old snow left
over in shaded areas of the high mountains, dirty
with earth and gravel. Now it was icy cold, and the
crystals slapped against the rocks and stung their
eyes. Herded together, the goats reached the forest,
arriving safely under the green boughs of the
moss-laden pines. But someone had gotten there
before them! A hare, recently changed into his
white winter coat, had also come down from the
peaks. He had spent the warm season there in his
home under some roots whose color resembled that
of his summer coat.

At the goat's arrival the hare excitedly wiggled
his nose and twitched his ears, for he was a timid
creature frightened by the slightest sound. Actually,
he had nothing to fear from his visitors; they
wouldn't pay any more attention to him now than
they had during the summer when their paths

chanced to cross up in the mountains. For the hare,
there would always be plenty to eat: he could nibble on the alder shoots or dig for roots with his
hard claws (providing the ground wasn't frozen
hard). And, if nothing else remained, as a last resort
there were always pine needles to nibble on. A diet
of pine needles would make his flesh taste like
turpentine—a fact that unfortunately would not de-
ter his bitterest enemy, the stoat. This wickedest
member of the weasel family, which also includes the
marten, pine marten and weasel, was always on the
lookout for a meal, ready and eager to sink his
thirty-four needle-sharp teeth into the neck of some
unsuspecting rabbit or hare. As a matter of fact,
the stoat wouldn't hesistate to attack even in broad
daylight, for thanks to his white coat, he remained
almost invisible in the snow. But the hare was used
to living dangerously, and he too could barely be
detected in the surrounding blanket of immaculate
white. Only the dark tips of his quivering ears revealed his presence.

The hare knew that for him death could also
come from above—perhaps in the form of an eagle,
or one of the few hungry vultures in the neighborhood. Luckily, when this king of the skies, the eagle,
passed over, he was already well hidden. Another
gust of wind raised more flurries of snow and the
gray clouds drifted on.

Winter had come to the mountains.

Stoat

DECEMBER

The Salmons' Great Adventure

Ingenious "ladders" enable salmon to get around dams.

Only a tiny spring can spread out to make a little pond and then, given time, turn into a babbling brook, the kind around which royal-coated ermines stealthily stalk before suddenly dashing off into the undergrowth like other members of the weasel family.

In these occasional pools the water is so still that you can plainly see every rock and multicolored pebble on its bottom. Now, in December, a thin film of ice may form on the surface, but underneath it the clear, cool waters will continue to flow.

And that is just as well, for it means that the fox will still be able to catch a tiny trout or two, and the stream's real wealth, its store of pearly salmon eggs, will be able to survive the winter. Just heavy enough to withstand the current's pull, the eggs will lie there on the river bottom until the spring thaw warms them enough to hatch.

What a fantastic adventure is in store for the denizens of the rivers and streams. By May, bare two months after they have hatched, the fingerlings are already carnivorous little brown fish darting hither and yon with the speed of light in search of drowned flies. And come May, the mayflies will be swarming in incredible numbers over the pools, to the delight of all the little trout and future salmon.

Twenty months will pass in this fashion, during which the parr, as they're known at that stage, will increase in strength and size (up to 8 inches) in preparation for their great adventure.

Then, all together, they will depart from their native waters, all their heads pointed upstream, letting the swift current carry them from stream to river and from river into the seas. There they linger a while, getting accustomed to the taste of salt water, until, still in a group, they disappear into the ocean.

Growth stages of a salmon

But their incredible odyssey is just beginning. Next summer, about mid-July, some of them will reappear at the river mouths. Others will wait three or four years; by this time they'll be magnificent fish, blue-sided and pink-bellied, almost three feet long and weighing up to thirty-five pounds! At this point they'll be robust enough to swim against even the strongest current, and will be able to leap right over dams and falls without needing to make use of the salmon ladders built to assist them on the fantastic journey.

For they remain dedicated to their goal, though their trip upstream may take as long as a year. During this entire period they will fast completely, living off the layers of fine fat that they acquired in the ocean depths. Once they finally reach their spawning ground—which will be the exact spot where they were born—they will be mere shadows of their former selves.

Yet all their efforts will have been successful, for there, where they were born, they will leave their own eggs before dying in their turn and being swept downstream by the river's flow. It is said that some recover once they have reached the sea again, but for most the sole purpose of their long struggle was simply to deposit a thousand red, translucent pearls on the stream's sandy bottom so that, the following spring, the salmon's great adventure may start all over again.

141

The Winter Birds' Cafeteria

To go outside on a winter's day may seem point‐
less and unappealing: it's cold and wet, the trees are
bare and leafless, and there's very little to see—or
so you say.

But have you really looked?

Let's take a walk through the pleasant hedgelined
paths that crisscross the English countryside.

True, the sky is overcast and the wind is cold. But
look there, beside the road. That clump of holly
with its shiny green leaves bears a cluster of bright
red berries, and there on the other side are more
vermillion buttons flashing cordial invitations to the
hungry birds; these are the berries of the dog rose,
a thorn-studded vine that only last spring gleamed
with white and pink flowers. Farther along are more
red, cherrylike clusters; these are the fruit of the
rowan, known to many as the "birds' bread," and
there are still others on the hawthorn bushes.

Yes, the winter landscape is full of color for those
who know how to open their eyes. The spindle tree
proudly displays pretty pink berries, while both the
juniper and the blackthorn, or sloe, produce fruit
of a purplish blue.

How cleverly nature has arranged things! Just as
the colorful blooms of spring and summer flowers

Hawthorn

Dog rose

Holly

Rowan

are meant to attract the pollinating bees, so do winter fruits attract the birds who spread their seeds far and wide.

And so that the wintering birds may see them more clearly, they are all quite bright in contrast to the gloomy weather.

The famished birds dive down on the berries, tearing them apart or swallowing them whole, depending on the size of their beaks; these berries are particularly rich in the sugar and vitamins the birds need to see them through the winter. Having digested the fruit, the birds then fly off and deposit the seed, which of course will grow all the more easily as it is already naturally manured. Farmers who fertilize their fields to assure a fine harvest do no more than our little feathered friends, though the former think they are being "scientific."

In winter all nature rests. Plants and trees no longer need the bees and birds except to take care of the berries still hanging on their branches: a real self-service cafeteria for feathered folk.

In the gardens, blackbirds and thrushes feast on the blue berries of the mahonia and the purplish clusters on the acuba (both shrubs of the barberry family), to say nothing of other delicacies on the mountain ash, the evergreen thorn and the ivy on the wall.

When snow covers the countryside with its white mantle, the work is almost done, though even in the depths of winter, birds can still manage to find a few holly or ivy berries to feed on here and there.

Now would be the perfect time to think of the little birds who creep timorously up to our houses and fly past our windows or perch on our windowsills. Let us hang a bit of suet in a nearby tree so the blue tit, or his cousin the coal tit, or that gallant fellow the robin can have a little something to eat. And let's throw out a few bread crumbs to the sparrows—they'll welcome anything—and some seed for the pigeons in the park and the blackbirds whose dark feathers seem even blacker now that they perch on snow-topped statues.

Spindle tree

Juniper

Blackthorn

DECEMBER

The Wolf Who Cried

He wasn't from the Hungarian plains, this wolf, nor from Poland or the Carpathian Mountains of central Europe. Nor had he crossed the Pyrenees from Spain during this horrible winter when both man and beast suffered so from the cold.

Instead, this lone wolf had come all the long way from the Abruzzi Mountains in Italy where he had once led a pack.

He was the only one left out of a pack that once hunted there, and though his flanks were lean and his tail dragged on the ground, his jaws were as strong as ever. And how well he'd have liked to clamp them together on something, because for days now he had been wandering like a gray ghost through the inhospitable brushland of the Cantal region in southern France without a bite to eat.

He'd have been content with anything at all—a little bird grabbed from under a pine's low-hanging branches, a few snails, a lost dog or a hare (though hares are always careful to keep out of sight). Sadly, all that he could see around him on the meager pastures was snow and more snow, and in the distance the barren hills that he'd just walked across, leaving a trail of dark prints in the all-enveloping white.

From time to time, he'd see a wisp of smoke in the freezing air, marking the location of a little lost hamlet, but he dare not approach anything smelling of man. Too recently in the Abruzzi Mountains he had only escaped men's guns by a miracle when he and his brood had come too close to a sheepfold.

Wearily he sat on his haunches and raised his head to the gray sky, letting forth a blood-curdling cry that made the most intrepid hunter quake.

Suddenly, an answering call resounded from across the wooded slopes, and the old wolf recog

Where did this lone wolf, now roaming through the woods, come from? Could he be from Hungary, Poland, Italy—or perhaps the distant Carpathian Mountains?

...ized the cry of a young wolf bitch. The bristles ...ose on the back of his neck. If his hearing and ...een sense of smell hadn't deceived him, there was ...ertainly a young female not far away. But though ...e had been strong and fearless while with the ...ack, his current solitude had made him cautious, ...ven cowardly.

Peering through the dark, he watched and waited apprehensively, his teeth bared.

Here she came at last, a sleek, playful creature, who from the odor of carrion on her breath had obviously spent the last few days tearing at the flesh and gnawing the bones of some unfortunate stray animal. At first the old wolf growled sullenly as she circled him like a friendly puppy, then suddenly he

licked her face with his tongue—the wolf's way of getting acquainted. He wasn't alone any more!

Together they trotted off into the night. Though they would spend some time up in the rough country dotted with briar and stunted juniper bushes, they wouldn't stay long enough in any one place for their presence to be noticed. If need be, they could easily travel up to sixty miles a day. And that would be just as well if they expected to raise a fine family of wolf cubs in some hidden den one day.

Wolves are rare in France nowadays, and those few that do exist live well out of men's ways. Little Red Riding Hood can go safely to Grandmother's, for neither she nor her grandmother stand much risk of being eaten up by those long, sharp fangs.

...uropean wolves and jackal (center)

Wintering in the Alps

An icy gale blows down the mountainside. Way up in the Gran Paradiso game reserve on the Italian slopes of the Alps, the animals sleep away, safely hidden in the dark forests. For some time now the inquisitive marmots have lain slumbering in their warm, hay-lined underground lairs.

At this altitude only the ibex, or wild goat, can face the rigorous winter. Perched on a rocky outcrop between two patches of snow, they peacefully bask in the thin December sun.

Every day, at the very same hour, they leave their shelter beneath an overhanging crag in search of their beloved "oline" grass. Although the grass is dry and tough now, it's all the ibex will have to live on through the winter, except for a few wisps of moss and lichen. With their huge ringed horns curving backward over their heads like swords, the ibex stride solemnly forward, scraping at the snow with their sharp hooves and then taking their ease on the rocks as the sun circles the horizon.

146

Yellow violet   *Centaurea*   *Gentian*

Having eaten very well all summer and fall, by now they have acquired thick coats and a solid layer of fat to protect them from the elements, and they seem quite unaffected by the bitter weather.

The mother ibex usually have only their kids for company, since the old bucks prefer the solitary splendor of some rocky outcrop from which they can survey the surrounding mountains. But now that there is no danger, and so no need to spread the alarm by scraping with their hooves, they too have condescended to rejoin the herd.

When the first warm breath of spring is felt and the chamois and the hare leave the woods for the high Alpine pastures, the "Steinbocks," or rock goats (as the Germans call them), climb ever higher, outdistancing all but the most intrepid climbers. Their amber-yellow eyes look disdainfully down on the lush meadows below where yellow violets, centaurea, gentian and other spring flowers dot the green grass.

By summertime, the male ibex can be glimpsed high above, their feet joined together, balanced on a dizzying pinnacle of rock. Their thick bodies and short legs keep them from being as elegant as their cousins the chamois, but for agility and staying power, they have no peer. Luckily, those huge horns are hollow inside; if they were solid, their weight might throw the ibex off balance and send him crashing down the mountainside!

Though it's barely half past two in the afternoon, here, high on the Alpine glaciers, the sun is already setting. It is time for the herd to be on its way. Those ibex who have been lying on the rocks slowly get up, and we can watch the spots of brown inching their way down the white slopes until they are swallowed by deepening shadows. As night falls they will find shelter under some overhanging rock. Down in the valleys below, the lights go on one by one, and the first stars add the enchantment of a Christmas card.

147

DECEMBER

Pathways in the Snow

When winter's frozen breath covers the countryside and the crows sit alone on barren branches, even the black grouse of the Scottish and Irish moors must make an effort to survive. Now the pink, heather-clad hills interspersed with salmon-filled lakes are silent and covered with snow.

The hunting season is over, and the cocks can breathe a little easier, though life is far from easy during the long, cold winters. Like its close cousin the ptarmigan, the black grouse's legs are entirely covered with downy feathers. (It is this feature that gives the ptarmigan its Latin name, *Lagopus,* which means "hare-legged.") How convenient this is for a northern bird who must make his way through snowdrifts without sinking in (and, in fact, the mountain hares also have snowshoe-like feet to help them along).

The grouse have developed a curious trick of ploughing pathways through the snow, and this enables them to keep well hidden from foxes and other predators (for men are not the only ones to appreciate their delicate flesh). From mid-flight, they can fall like rocks into the deep snow, leaving not the slightest tell-tale trace.

Despite the only moderate warmth of their plumage, grouse can live comfortably through the winter,

Black grouse (male)

though like all other wild things, their diet is apt to be meager, consisting of nothing more than a few roots, insects and larvae. Nevertheless, they can survive until the spring fogs come again to throw their wispy shadows across the land. Then it will be April, and time to dance and strut in order to attract a harem of hens (whom they will quickly leave again to bring up the young chicks alone).

The capercaillie has more or less the same habits, but what a difference in size. With a wingspan of 5 feet and weighing almost 20 pounds, he is a magnificent bird indeed. The sight of him showing off his huge, turkeylike tail before a covey of hens, puffing out his chest and stamping his feet on the ground as he drags his wings, is well worth waiting for. He will work his way around his chosen nesting ground, stamp his feet as if half demented and jump quickly to a tree stump to call out a series of "tick-up, tick-ups," followed by a pop like a champagne cork coming out of a bottle. His buff-colored lady friends encourage all this with raucous cries, and the entire spectacle is well worth recording on film or tape.

Ptarmigan

But who will dig out ant eggs, insects and the
ew tender cranberries to feed the capercaille's
icks?

Not the irascible old cock, naturally! He is a
ne individualist at heart, a lover of lonely heaths
nd moors cut by quick-flowing streams, of rocky
aces and pine forests. When the first snow falls he
ill not carve out pathways in the snow, but will
rch in a pine tree, slowly devouring its needles
nd when they are gone, making do with the bark
self). But when spring comes again and the chicks
e hatched, when the sage trembles beside the

burns and abundance is in the air, he will vary his
menu by gobbling down all the buds and berries he
can find.

As for the black grouse, many are still to be
found in the Tyrolean and Bavarian Alps of Austria
and Germany, and many of their lyre-shaped tails
are used to decorate local hats whether the owners
are hunters or not. Like Scotland's red grouse, they
carve tunnels in the snow, preferably among the
birch forests where they are sure to find their favorite foods, the buds of young rhododendron and fine
ripe whortleberries.

apercaillie

Crossbill

Blue tit

Christmas Eve

Whole truckloads of pine and spruce trees have come down from the mountains and the air is full of the penetrating smell of fresh resin.

Up among the giant trees which remain uncut, the crossbills peck away at the tawny cones.

It is Christmastime.

As the wind slips through the reeds beside the pond, a little blue tit bores a hole in one of the frozen stalks with his pointed beak. He is trying to extract a tiny spider which is seeking shelter from the winter's blast within the hollow stem.

In our barren gardens, the blackbirds hop here and there while a thrush pecks avidly at rotten apples forgotten on the ground. Four bullfinches leave the cherry tree after they have cut off a few of the early buds.

Thrush

Moorhen

Christmas rose

Perhaps we, too, should follow the Swedish custom of hanging little sheaves of grain on the trees for our springtime songsters, never forgetting that birds and flowers are nature's ornaments during the fine weather. But nature too must rest, and the winter frost helps kill off some of the vermin buried in the soil. Of course, there will always be enough for avid beaks and scratching claws when the lark once again soars into the blue and fills our ears with his springtime song.

The hungry sparrows glean what they can from an overturned garbage can (watched all the while by the cat who is warmly ensconced behind a nearby window pane).

But what color can the garden supply? For one, a superb display of hellbore, or Christmas roses, white petals tinged with pink. And there, to one side, providing the autumn has not been too cruel, a few pansies and primroses.

Lights twinkle from every house, the streets are decorated and the shop windows are filled with toys. What a wonderful time of year it is for people—and above all, for children. But what of our friends the animals?

Think of the frozen mist that settles in drops on the backs of the deer in the forests and on the mountainside. Think of the moorhens and ducks gliding around on the icy surfaces of ponds in search of a little clear water. December nights are long, and the darkness falls early at this time of year.

The animals forget their rivalries and huddle together to share the warmth that no living thing (except the fish, of course) can do without. Together they search for every little bit of life-giving food. "Twitt-twitt!" A robin chirps on the end of a barren twig. Proudly puffing out his little red breast and fluffing his feathers against the cold, he sings despite the winter weather—and then quickly hops off to see if anyone has left him a few crumbs.

It's Christmastime!

INDEX

Index